£1·30

CONTENTS

The Topical Times FOOTBALL BOOK

D. C. Thomson & Co. Ltd.,
London—Manchester
Glasgow—Dundee

*All first-person articles as told to
" Topical Times Football Book " writers*

The Human Catapult

BENT like a bow, Kilmarnock's IAN JARDINE winds himself up for something extra special in the long throw line. His target — and he always makes it — is the far-off figure with the udraised arm.

That was just one of the dramatic off-field happenings the crowd never see.

*   *   *   *

An equally dramatic square-up between manager and players took place before a Scottish Cup-tie between Dumbarton and Hearts.

Hearts players demanded a bigger win bonus with half to be paid for a draw. The previous arrangement had been no win, no bonus. Strike action was threatened if the demands were not met.

Hearts' manager Willie Ormond was furious. But eventually, only an hour before kick-off, the matter was resolved.

The bonus remained the same—but half would be paid for a draw. The result—Hearts achieved a draw, but lost the replay at home!

WE WON'T PLAY UNLESS.....

JOHN GIDMAN
— one inch from disaster

Another dressing-room incident came within an ace of being a disaster.

John Gidman, Aston Villa and England right-back, was rushed to hospital by police car after cutting his wrist opening a window.

It happened in the dressing-room at Norwich. The window was stuck by paint. Gidman tapped it and it shattered.

Said Gidman: " It was a shocking cut. I was told at the hospital I was just an inch away from severing an artery, and the same distance from cutting tendons."

*   *   *   *

There are also some dressing-room upsets which can be of benefit to a club.

Take Bolton Wanderers. Their promotion to Division One two years ago can perhaps be traced to a pre-season row in a German dressing-room.

Says Wanderers' skipper Roy Greaves, " I've only seen our manager Ian Greaves lose his temper once and that was on our tour of West Germany.

" We were two goals up against a team of amateurs and lost 3-2.

" The boss came into our dressing-room at the end, slammed the door and said, ' All of you shut up and listen to me.'

" He gave us a real rollicking. I thought at one stage he was going to thump us.

" When we returned home the boss worked us really hard. The benefit was shown in our promotion push that term."

Just another off-the-field incident that can be just as dramatic as anything that happens in the game itself.

JIM PLATT, Middlesbrough goalkeeper, is one of the nice guys of football. But that didn't stop him getting mixed up in a sensational dressing-room blow-up before an important game.

It happened this way . . .

Middlesbrough were playing Everton at Goodison Park. The then 'Boro manager, Jack Charlton, delivering his pre-match team talk, gave instructions to Jim Platt on positioning at corner-kicks.

But Jim disagreed with Big Jack and a few heated words were exchanged. Charlton soon settled the argument. He pointed to reserve 'keeper, Pat Cuff.

" Right, Pat, you'll be in goal for this one!"

So when Middlesbrough went out Pat Cuff was in Jim Platt's place.

CORNERED!

Placing the ball —
Q.P.R.'s so talented
STAN BOWLES

ALL GO FOR JOE

Manchester City's
JOE CORRIGAN
finds it's mighty hectic
being a goalie.

ME & MY SEVEN BOSSES

They gave me a blueprint for the future says BOBBY GOULD

AFTER 16 good years in football I hope I'm not finished as a player.

But, as assistant-manager/player coach with Mike Bailey at Hereford, I'm starting out on what I hope will be a happy managerial career.

I believe I have the perfect grounding . . .

As a player I've had the luck to learn from some top managers—Jimmy Hill, Bertie Mee, Bill McGarry, Ron Greenwood and Don Howe among them.

I have tried to pick out their best ideas and qualities for my own use as a manager.

Like Jimmy Hill's flair for publicity. Or Bertie Mee's wonderful calmness and organising ability. Bill McGarry's honesty and will-to-win. Ron Greenwood's technical knowledge. Alan Dicks' business-sense. Don Howe's coaching skill.

I have enjoyed working with every manager—despite their different approaches.

Jimmy Hill was perhaps the greatest all-round boss I've come across.

What a fantastic job he did for Coventry City! He transformed a struggling Third Division side into a top-class First Division outfit.

I remember Jimmy saying to the chairman when he took over . . . "Within five years I'll have you in the First Division."

And he did it!

' J.H. '—that was the way he had his players address him—was appointed manager just after we'd lost to non-league King's Lynn in the F.A. Cup.

The club was down in the dumps. But J.H. had an eye for publicity. He could make a good story for the newspapers out of anything.

Suddenly it was Coventry City this, Coventry City that every day in the papers. The players began to believe the club meant something.

Another outstanding memory of Jimmy Hill is of the year we won promotion to the First Division. I was top scorer with 24 goals in 38 games.

Come the day, I went to see him about my new contract for the First Division. I was on £32.00 a week at the time.

" I'll give you £40.00 a week," he said.

" I want £45.00," I replied.

He said £40 was his final offer, but I persisted with £45.00.

" Right, you're on the transfer list." said Jimmy.

For the next couple of days I scoured the papers in vain for any mention of my position. So I went back in to see J.H.

" There's nothing in the papers about me being transfer listed. What's it all about?" I asked him.

" How much do you want?" replied J.H.

" £45."

" I'll give you £42.10s. (£42.50)"

" I'll take it." I said.

" Good," replied Jimmy.

J.H. knew what he was doing!

Just a few weeks later we were all called to a meeting in his office.

" I've decided I no longer want my future decided by the results achieved by 11 other people between 3.00 and 5.00 on a Saturday afternoon. I'm resigning," said Jimmy.

ALAN DICKS

BOBBY CAMPBELL

DON HOWE

BILL McGARRY

"SCORE GOALS AND NO MESSING ABOUT"

For most of us it was a bombshell. We'd just won promotion. The club was booming. Everyone had tremendous faith in J.H. Everything he'd done at Coventry had gone right. There seemed no limit to what we could achieve.

Later I'd learned he'd wanted the security of a ten-year contract from the club—and they wouldn't give him it. So J.H. moved into television to earn more than he'd asked from Coventry.

From Coventry I moved to Arsenal. Their manager, Bertie Mee, was totally different from J.H. Bertie shunned personal publicity and hadn't been a well-known player.

It was only after I left Arsenal that I fully appreciated the talents of Bertie Mee. He was a genius at organisation. Superb at man management. Bertie knew exactly what his own limits were and how to get the most out of other people.

I had an indifferent spell at Arsenal, although I became a far better player. I improved my work-rate, and learned how to use my left foot. But I lost the knack of scoring goals.

Eventually I moved on to Wolves and Bill McGarry, the most honest manager I've ever played for.

"I've looked at your record. I've watched you play. And if I see you in our half of the field I'll kick your backside." he told me. "I want you to score goals and no messing about."

McGarry was so straightforward. I always knew where I was with Bill. I enjoyed playing for him.

While I was with Wolves, Don Howe moved from Arsenal to take over as manager of West Brom. "That's one club I won't be joining," I said to my wife Marjorie.

I didn't think my record with Arsenal was good enough to impress Don. But soon he was in touch with Wolves to buy me, and I became his first signing for West Brom!

From The Hawthorns I went to Bristol City and Alan Dicks. 'A.D.' to his players, following the example of Coventry, where he was coach with Jimmy Hill.

I admired A.D.'s financial skill. The club was pretty small-time when he joined, but he carried them through a difficult period. Juggling the transfer market to make ends meet, he still produced a promotion winning side.

I wasn't too happy at Bristol City, and Norwich manager Ron Saunders wanted to sign me. It was all fixed, though Ron warned me his own position was not very secure.

I spoke to him on a Thursday, and agreed to sign on the Monday. On Saturday night I heard Norwich had lost at home and Ron was out of a job. He told me Norwich still wanted me, but also mentioned West Ham might be interested.

Sure enough Ron Greenwood approached Bristol for me. I travelled up to meet him at White Hart Lane, where West Ham had a youth match against Spurs.

Ron and I sat throughout chatting about the game. He asked how I would feel joining the club with players like Bobby Moore & Co. Whether I thought I would fit in with such big name men and so on.

I told them I had no fears and agreed to join them.

Next to my first club, Coventry, West Ham will always have a special place in my heart.

HAT-TRICK START

I learned more about the techniques of football in my spell with them than in my previous entire career. At one stage I had 15 consecutive matches on the subs' bench without getting on to the pitch. But I was always learning.

From West Ham I went back to Wolves and Bill McGarry.

Then—on to Bristol Rovers. I had kept my home in Bristol from my days at Ashton Gate, so it was a great move in that respect.

Don Megson signed me. I scored a hat-trick in my first match. The following week we were smashed 9—0 at Tottenham! You can't get much more of a constrast than that!

Bobby Campbell took over when Don moved to America, and I became a player-coach. Bobby believed in the old-fashioned style of play with wingers, and it was successful.

I got to appreciate the use of wingers at Bristol before leaving to join Mike Bailey at Hereford.

So now I can look back and hope to adapt what I've learned from the different managers. But I'll still do things my way!

JIMMY HILL

BERTIE MEE

11

RON GREENWOOD

PUZZLE SPOT

LETTER LINKS

Start at the top left-hand corner and then move down, across or diagonally to spot seven players.

S	I	S	R	E	N	M	I	N	U
E	O	R	A	L	A	N	N	C	Y
S	N	U	H	O	S	H	G	R	T
C	S	P	N	L	I	L	N	G	A
O	P	E	L	W	K	I	S	H	E

NAME GAME

Spot the football personalities from these clues.
1 Arsenal's admiral.
2 Ipswich's sailor.
3 Leeds' man from a Scottish island.
4 Liverpool's road man.
5 Manchester United's man from the Middle East.
6 Nottingham Forest's poet.
7 Stoke boss from South Africa.
8 Is he safe as a house with Spurs?
9 He's very mobile with Wolves.
10 Partick Thistle's golf hazard.
11 Glasgow Rangers' barrel maker.

SPOT THE TEAM

See how few clues you need to spot this team—
1—They were formed in 1878 and first played at Stanley Park.
2—They won the First Division championship for the first time in 1890-91 and last won it in 1969-70.
3—They won the F.A. Cup the same year as England won the World Cup.
4—One of their players holds the individual record of 60 goals in one season in the First Division.
5—They are known as the Toffeemen.
6—They now play at Goodison Park.

FACE NAME

Who is the famous player whose surname consists of these letters?

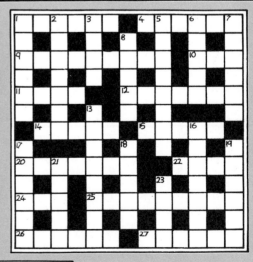

WORD PYRAMID

Complete this pyramid with the help of NORWICH. Here are the clues.

1 A famous football stand.
2 Rodney of England.
3 Middlesbrough and Scotland goalkeeper.
4 Where Greenock Morton play.
5 The oldest club in the Football League.
6 Where the Wanderers may come to roost.

N
O
R
W
I
C
H

SPOT THE CLUES

Re-arrange the letters shown below and you'll spot the names of six football clubs.

1—BEHNORRSSTUWWY
2—AABDEEHIKLMNOSTTW
3—CCDEEEHILNORSTTU
4—ABCGHIIIMMMNRTY
5—AACCEHHILLNORTTT
6—ACDEENOORRRSSTV

CROSSWORD

Across.
1 Sounds like a well-built Ipswich defender. (6) 4 Counter-balance. (6) 9 They play at Filbert Street. (9) 10 For example, training might annoy. (3) 11 Gary's ex-City now Albion. (4) 12 Peter's got a household name. (7) 14 Did he used to steal a goal for West Brom and England? (5) 15 Opponent mostly an Italian internationalist. (5) 20 A road taken by Ipswich fans?. (7) 22 A favourite at the Lido? (4) 24 Kenny Dalglish's favourite colour? (3) 25 Some referees make themselves thus. (9) 26 Hop over to try for one! (6) 27. Badges. (6)

Down.
1 Wanderers. (6) 2 Reds may air their attacking prowess. (7) 3 Level. (4) 5 Hurried help on the pitch. (5-3) 6 A mighty man for Swansea? (5) 7 Ken's to collect them for the cup final tickets. (6) 8 Victory at Victoria is their aim. (5) 13 The Pilgrims. (8) 16 A Tottenham import. (7) 17 Gusto. (6) 18 Easy chances. (5) 19 Does Al worry the Rams? (6) 21 On which you can hear game commentary.(5) 23 Incentive for a London player? (4)

ANSWERS ON PAGE 116

STEVE PERRYMAN
Spurs

THEY CALL ME— LEATHER LUNGS LANGLEY

RELEGATION to the Second Division made last season a disaster for Chelsea. But one game stands out for me personally.

That was at Middlesbrough. Right, we were beaten 7—2, but it was also the day I achieved my ambition—by playing alongside Peter Osgood.

Since I was a toddler I've been a Chelsea fanatic. My parents took me to Stamford Bridge almost as soon as I could walk.

When I was old enough to appreciate what the game was all about I knew the kind of player I wanted to become—a Peter Osgood. To me Ossie was the King of Chelsea.

TOMMY LANGLEY, Chelsea

I wrote to Chelsea when I was 10 years old asking for a trial. Later I came up from my home in Basingstoke twice a week for the schoolboy training sessions at Stamford Bridge.

All the time I was hoping to become another Peter Osgood, and play centre-forward for Chelsea. When Ossie scored vital goals in the F.A. Cup final (the replay against Leeds) and in the European Cup Winners' Cup (Real Madrid), I couldn't have been happier.

It was a terrible blow to me when he left Chelsea in 1974 to join Southampton. Still a junior at Stamford Bridge, my ambition to play with Peter Osgood seemed to have gone.

But, early last season, it became a possibility when he rejoined Chelsea. So, that game at Middlesbrough was magic for me and my family—despite the result.

Since he returned to Stamford Bridge Peter Osgood has helped me a lot—especially with ball control.

Long ago I realised I would never be really like Osgood. My style is completely different. Ossie relies on superb control and flair. My assets are stamina and strength.

But Peter has helped improve my control. He emphasised the value of 'one touch' technique. Control the ball with the first touch, and the second is easy.

FAMILY OF FANS

NOW we are back in the Second Division crowds at Stamford bridge are naturally smaller. But there will always be one group of fans—my family. My parents, grandparents, aunts and uncles all support Chelsea.

I'll always remember my first match. I was only 16, given my chance in the First Division against Leicester City at home.

I didn't have time to get nervous, I was too busy rushing round organising tickets for the family. The office staff winced when I said I wanted 33. But Secretary Chris Matthews did a great job for me. I got all my relations in.

Nowadays there are not so many. But my family fan club still turns up for every match. Their support means a lot to me.

It's the kind of backing our Yugoslavian goalkeeper, Petar Borota, will never be able to get in England. But he's such a character, he gets all the fans on his side anyway.

Petar is a great guy to have in the dressing room.

Last season, at one time, we went 13 games without a win—and Petar played in 11 of them. That was before dropping out to allow Peter Bonetti to complete his 600 league matches for Chelsea.

In the first game without him we beat Middlesbrough. Petar was the first man in the dressing room at the end, shaking hands with everybody in sight.

" You play good—me no play." he said.

He was happy for the lads. That kind of spirit has made Petar one of the most popular players at Chelsea.

Of course he took a lot of ribbing from the players on first arrival. He didn't know much English, so we told him what to say at certain times. Occasionally slipping in the wrong word for a laugh. There were some hilarious moments.

But this man from Yugoslavia could take the joke. And he learned fast.

His determination for fitness once shook Eamonn Bannon. For at four o'clock one morning, Eamonn was awakened in his hotel room by a strange noise—and discovered Petar—doing press-ups on the floor!

CHELSEA'S NON-STOP NINETY MINUTE MAN TELLS HIS STORY

It's quite something to watch him in the dressing room before a match. He warms up like a boxer. Shadow punching, exercising, jumping, skipping. Everything to make sure he's really supple before going out.

Our five-a-side training games are a great favourite with him. He plays like a defender, tackling and heading and going upfield. Maybe he'll break out in a league game one day.

Yes, Petar works hard at his game, and that's something that was always drummed into me by my father—a boxer when he was young.

He was a good amateur. When he turned professional he was too happy-go-lucky to get anywhere. All along he has wanted to make sure I didn't make the same mistake.

As a teenager I was all for going out with the other lads and having a good time. My dad kept on at me to stay home and get early nights.

At the time this got me down. But Dad was right. I kept my natural fitness. My stamina is one of my assets.

I'm not the quickest player at Chelsea. Clive Walker and Lee Frost can leave me behind. But, after three or four runs, I still have my pace. I can wear down defenders. They might be quicker at the start. By the end I have the edge.

That's why they call me " Lungs " at Chelsea. I'm usually still going strong while the others are gasping for breath. They reckon I've got leather lungs.

One of the most powerful players I've come across is Paul Mariner of Ipswich, whom I met on the England ' B ' trip to New Zealand a year or two back.

Paul has skill as well. I rate him a top all round striker. He helped me a lot on the tour. As did experienced men like Joe Corrigan, Viv Anderson and Dave Needham. I was just a kid called in as a replacement for the injured David Geddis. But they were all ready to rally round.

I've been in the Chelsea squad for five years. But I'm still only 21, with a lot to learn.

I'm also finding League football much tougher now. I think it's because, at 16 or 17, I was too young to know what the game was all about. Cente-halves gave me plenty of space and time to run because they could always steer me into the areas they wanted me to be in.

They didn't need to try anything very physical because I wasn't too much of a danger. Although I did score the winner as a substitute against Birmingham City on my 17th birthday.

I began to think first team football was easy after the hectic pace of reserve and youth team games. Now I know better.

In the penalty-box, where it matters, you get no time at all.

Although last season was bad for Chelsea, I was reasonably happy with my scoring. I finished with about a third of the team's total. A fair percentage for any striker.

Since Danny Blanchflower took over the side we have been gradually changing style. It wasn't easy last season. We were caught at times between two different patterns of play.

Now we are ironing out a lot of our problems.

It's hard for a newcomer to fit straight in. No matter whether he's player or manager. A team has its own kind of language and " in-jokes " and it takes a while to understand them.

We have the usual nicknames at Chelsea. Big Micky Droy is " The Whale ". Gary Stanley is " Senor " because he's dark like a Spaniard. Ron Harris is " Buller ". Ian Britton is named " Tattoo " after the little fellah in the television series " Fantasy Island ".

Whatever we're called we have Chelsea at heart. With the aim, this season, of getting back in the First Division.

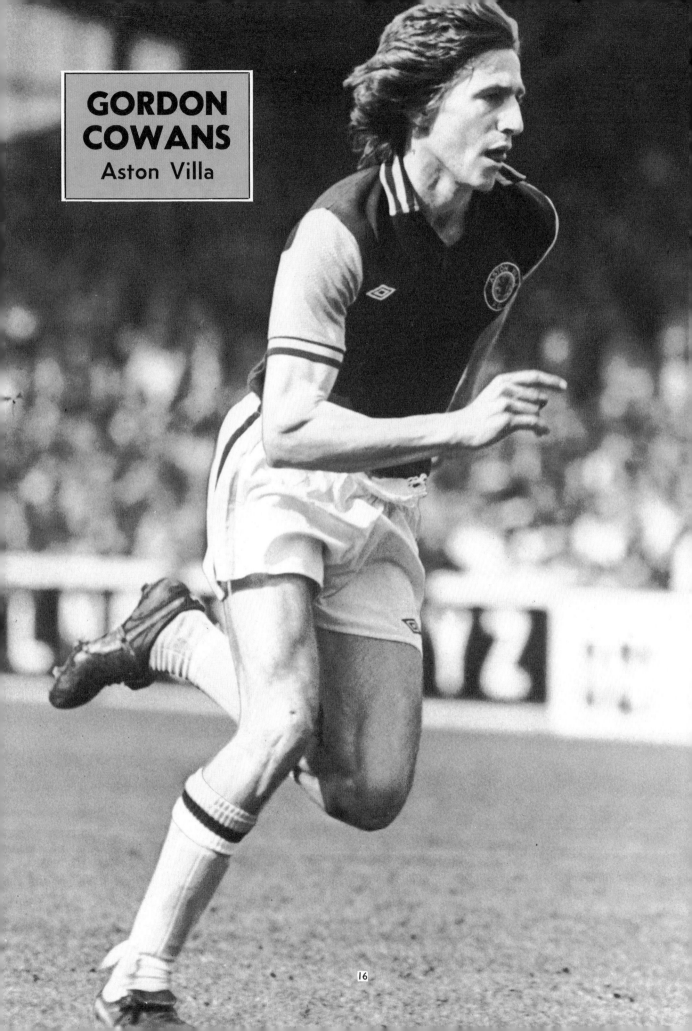

GORDON COWANS
Aston Villa

16

GOAL GRABBER

Arsenal paid £250,000 to sign ALAN SUNDERLAND from Wolves and it's been money well spent. Many a vital goal has been notched by this aggressive raider.

TRANSFER BOMBSHELL
from my landlady

THE Old Trafford loudspeakers reeled off the Manchester United side—name by name. Finally came . . . " Number Eleven . . . Mike Thomas ". The 52,000 crowd roared their approval. The Stretford End fans chanted my name.

That was the welcome I got when making my home debut against Spurs after my £300,000 move from Wrexham.

What a moment. I felt really great!

It was a far cry from the loudspeaker messages that reached me when I was at High School in Colwyn Bay.

I was never one for school work. In fact I played truant many, many times.

When the other lads were doing treble maths or woodwork, I would be doing treble football!

The school tannoy system would send out the message " Would Michael Thomas please report to the headmaster's office?"

The head would ask me where I had been instead of doing my lessons. I always told him I had been out playing football. He was on my side and would reply—" Good lad, keep it up." Then he'd pat me on the head and let me go.

MIKE THOMAS

Obviously he thought even then I could make the grade as a footballer. I have since been back to the school to give the headmaster one of my Welsh international shirts.

We were a football-mad family. I would play in the street until it was pitch dark. Just knocking the ball against the fence. With my brothers I played a lot of " keepie-up."

Brother Kevin had a trial with Blackburn Rovers. Philip was supposed to have a week's trial with West Ham United. But he came back from London after only a day!

I was the only one in our family who eventually made the grade. Maybe because it was the only thing I ever wanted to do—or could have done!

Manchester United's
MIKE THOMAS
Tells His Story

As a kid I spent all my pocket money on football magazines and annuals. I still buy them now if I'm in them! It's nice to read about yourself, and a bit special to see a picture with ' MIKE THOMAS . . . MANCHESTER UNITED AND WALES ' underneath it.

Although I'm a Manchester United player now, the team I idolised as a boy was Everton.

With a few mates I'd get a lift to Goodison Park from Colwyn Bay. Our favourite spot was on the Gwladys Street terraces. My hero then was Alan Ball.

What impressed me about Alan was his confidence. When I made the Wrexham first team I was very unsure of myself.

Perhaps it was because I was only 17 but I would always pass to a more experienced player.

I lacked the confidence to hold the ball and try something on my own. As soon as I received it I would look for a way to get rid of it quickly!

It's a terrible problem to have. You'll never be a top-flight player if you don't have faith in your own ability.

However, the turning point came when I played for Wales against West Germany in 1977. My first " cap "!

I was on the left wing against the great Bertie

"LIFE OF LUXURY AT OLD TRAFFORD"

Vogts. I played really well and gave Vogts a bit of a runaround.

All the publicity and the fact the Welsh manager thought I was good enough for international football made me start to believe in myself.

TARGET – THE FIRST DIVISION

THE clincher came when Wrexham met Liverpool at the Racecourse Ground in the quarter final of the League Cup in January 1978.

Liverpool, European Cup holders, had a team packed with international players. I did well that night and realised I had enough ability to compete with the best players in the game.

At the start of the 1978-79 season I heard First Division clubs were interested in me.

I knew the First Division was where I wanted to play. I had set a target of being in the Wrexham first team by the time I was 17. I had done that, of course. I was aiming to be on the international scene for Wales by 20. And I was.

I decided that, at 24, I was ready to play First Division football. Wrexham had always been very good to me. I knew it would be a

SAMMY McILROY — top marks for skill

wrench to leave. It was such a friendly place.

My best mate at Wrexham was Joey Jones. He went to Liverpool in 1975. Everything was going well for him there. He picked up a League Championship and European Cup winners medals.

Then Joey lost his first team place and he reckoned there was no future for him at Liverpool. The only club he wanted to join was Wrexham. So he came back.

Joey warned me life in the First Division could be tough, but I knew I wouldn't be satisfied until I tried it for myself.

Aston Villa, Newcastle United and Middlesbrough were all interested. Then one day I went back to my digs above a coal merchants in Wrexham. My landlady was waiting for me.

She told me Arfon Griffiths, Wrexham's manager, had 'phoned. The message was that Manchester United wanted to sign me! I was to phone him back.

I was shaking with excitement when I phoned, Arfon told me that it looked as though I would be joining United that week!

I hardly slept a wink for three days until I passed my medical and finally signed for £300,000!

It was a tremendous feeling when I first pulled on a United shirt. That was in the Chelsea dressing-room. I sat in my kit looking round the room, bewildered. However the lads at Old Trafford soon made me feel part of the team.

The United player who has impressed me most is Sammy McIlroy. His work-rate and skill are tops. From the time I arrived Sammy helped me along.

Martin Buchan has really impressed me with his coolness in tight situations. His reading of the game and his passing are excellent.

The biggest difference between United and Wrexham is I don't have to clean my own boots or take my training kit home to be washed!

I reckon it is a luxury to arrive for training and find your kit all laid out. I know I have joined a great club. A look at the stadium and a taste of the atmosphere the Old Trafford crowd generates make you realise that.

I haven't lost all my ties with Wrexham, since Wales play most of their home matches on the Racecourse Ground.

When I join up with my Welsh party it gives me the chance to team up with Joey Jones again, and not just on the field either.

Joey and I are great practical jokers. We often buy rubber masks from joke-shops. It causes quite a bit of head-turning in hotels when we come down for dinner in the masks!

One of our favourite tricks is to phone a team-mate in the hotel, pretend we are from a National newspaper and conduct an interview.

I'm never too far away from Joey even when I'm at Old Trafford. In the Executive suite at the ground there are large photographs of United's F.A. Cup victory over Liverpool in 1977. Joey is on a few, so in the morning I always say " hello "!

Talking of FA Cup wins brings me back to the serious business. Obviously when you talk of ambition it means winning things.

I signed for Manchester United because I'm sure they're good enough to get among the trophies. I hope to do my bit to help them on the winning way!

And who knows—Ivor Allchurch's record number of 68 caps for Wales is still up for grabs!

MIKE ELWISS
Crystal Palace

20

JIMMY
NEIGHBOUR
Norwich City

21

MARK PROCTOR
Middlesbrough

RICCY
VILLA
SPURS

THE

Stars from
foreign parts who
made their mark
in Britain

KAZIMIERZ
DEYNA
*MANCHESTER
CITY*

OSVALDO
ARDILES
SPURS

INVADERS

FRANS
THIJSSEN
IPSWICH

ALEX
SABELLA
SHEFFIELD UNITED

ALBERTO
TARANTINI
BIRMINGHAM CITY

25

BIG DAY FOR THE

ALAN BUCKLEY —
*Striking for
Birmingham City*

NOVEMBER 18, 1978 was an ordinary Saturday in the Football League programme.

But two player brothers from Nottingham will long remember that date.

At the Baseball Ground, Derby, Alan and Steve Buckley met on a football field for the first time since they played in the same lads' club team ten years before.

The moment signified the Buckley family had made their mark in professional football. Steve's team, Derby County, were playing Alan's Birmingham City in a First Division game.

Alan, the elder, remembers the encounter with a tinge of regret.

"The only time I spoke to Steve was down by a corner flag," he says. "His socks were round his ankles, I told him he looked a real scruff.

"He replied minutes later by taking the ball the length of the field and cracking in a beauty to give Derby their winner."

The Buckleys had taken totally different paths to that meeting in last season's First Division.

Often it looked like they would never find themselves together at the game's highest level.

Starting as an apprentice with First Division Nottingham Forest, Alan dipped to the Third when he moved to Walsall. Finally he came back to the top flight when Birmingham paid £200,000 for him in October' 78.

Steve's route to the heights started in the East Midlands non-League set-up. There Luton Town picked him up and plunged him immediately into Division One action. Luton, relegated, sold left-back Steve to Derby County for £175,000.

NO FUTURE AT FOREST

AS it was, their paths might have crossed much earlier. Both could have been playing for the club they had supported as kids—Nottingham Forest.

Striker Alan takes up the story . . .

"I was on my way up through the Forest grades and the manager at the time, Johnny Carey, had Steve earmarked to follow in my footsteps.

"When 15, he turned down the chance to join Arsenal so he could be free for our local club. But when Matt Gillies became manager he took interest in Steve no further.

"Steve signed up with local non-League clubs and I found myself relegated from reserves to third team.

"Mr Gillies did give me my first team chance a short while later, but then the Forest management changed. Again it was a Buckley who suffered.

"I'd been making good progress but when Dave

BUCKLEY BOYS...

Mackay took over he dropped me, loaned me out to Walsall, and eventually sold me to the Fellows Park people.

"I had no regrets about dropping to Division Three. I saw there was no future for me at Nottingham.

"I aimed to make a name for myself by scoring a lot of goals. If I did, I knew I'd be on my way back to the First Division.

"It took me quite a long time to get my move. But eventually Jim Smith, the Birmingham boss, had the courage to shell out the money to buy me."

STEVE BUCKLEY—
Defending for Derby County

Whilst Alan's career was being rebuilt in Division Three, Steve was taking the fast lane to success.

He recalls, "After Forest turned me away I went part-time with clubs like Ilkeston and Burton.

"I had a dozen different jobs—working in a brickyard, as a plumber's mate, delivering beer and the like.

"Ever since Alan had made it as a pro I felt that was the life for me as well. When Luton gave me my chance I jumped at it.

"Despite my delayed entry into League football, I played my first Division One game at a younger age than Alan. I was 19, he was 20 when making his debut for Forest.

Both Buckley boys' parents have always provided support and encouragement.

As Steve says, "Mum and Dad used to go to all home games at Luton and to Walsall home matches.

"Both sets of fixtures always seemed to fit in with each other. Alan and I got tremendous encouragement from our parents being there.

"They still manage to see a good many of our matches. Derby is practically on the doorstep for them and Birmingham not so far away.

"We watch each other, too. Alan is a regular at the Baseball Ground when he isn't playing. I often make the trip to St. Andrew's."

But the brothers rarely discuss the problems of their respective clubs. In fact Alan tells me:

"We chat about the game for hours. But usually about other clubs and seldom about any difficulties either of us are having. We don't go into detail about future opponents."

The Buckleys learned their football on the recreation ground which backs on to their parents' home.

Steve recalls, "Alan and I, along with our dad, used to spend every spare minute on the 'rec'.

"From there we went on to play together for Eastwood Lads Club. I was left winger in those days, Alan was cracking in goals as a centre-forward."

And Alan confirms, "I was 14. Steve would have been 12. We also played together in a school under-12 team when I was ten and Steve eight. So it was clear we had football in our veins."

So, after plotting widely varying routes to their present success, Steve and Alan Buckley are at last hitting the same notes.

And that should mean many more red letter days for the family as the two face each other across the halfway line.

BILLY'S BLOCKBUSTER!

BILLY JENNINGS, West Ham United, fires a rocket shot at goal. Shooting power of the sort every keeper dreads — and the fans love to see.

28

ON CALL FOR ENGLAND!

Nottingham Forest's star trio, TONY WOODCOCK, PETER SHILTON and VIV ANDERSON, take time off from England training duty.

MACHINE-MADE GOALIE—

He Trains With A Robot

TWO thousand pounds of Swedish machinery helps keep Ipswich goalie, Paul Cooper, in tip-top shape.

Explains Paul . . .

"The inventor of a ball-firing machine presented one to the club. It's ideal for training. The machine can be set to fire balls high or low.

"I reckon all clubs should have one. They give keepers a good work-out. And it frees other players to do their own training, instead of having to feed the goalkeeper.

"After every game I go over my performance, analysing every goal I've lost. Then I work out what needs to be done. And that's when the ball machine comes in handy!"

Paul Cooper and the robot. Ready for a gruelling training session.

Loading the robot. The balls are fed into the machine.

The ball machine in action, forcing the keeper to full stretch.

ARCHIE GEMMILL
Nottingham Forest

MICK CHANNON
Manchester City

AUSTIN HAYES
Southampton

33

WALKABOUT

Stepping-out in style, the Bolton ball-jugglers go through their paces.

PAUL JONES, NEIL McNAB, DAVID BURKE, PETER NICHOLSON, ROY GREAVES,

34

JIM McDONAGH, FRANK WORTHINGTON, WILLIE MORGAN, NEIL WHATMORE.

STRANRAER F.C

THE DO-IT-YOURSELF CLUB

YOU get the feeling as you approach Stair Park that things at Stranraer Football Club are going to be just a little different.

Where else in Britain, for instance, would you have to pass a paddling pool, penguins and polar bears, swings and roundabouts, AND then go round the bandstand just to get to the ground?

You see it's within the town's recreation ground and children's corner.

But then everything about the little Wigtownshire club is out of the ordinary. Not least the fact they don't have a manager. And don't even want one.

The club is run by a twelve-man committee, who list plumbers, farmers, painters, and auctioneers among their members. They do everything from picking the team to manning the turnstiles.

Odd jobs about the ground? The committee will see to them as well.

NO SMOKING

THERE'S even a farmer who sows grass seed on the pitch every close season to make sure it's in tip-top shape at the kick-off each August.

The all-important team selection is made at the committee's weekly meeting every Monday night. Each member votes for his choice. The player with most votes out of twelve plays on the Saturday. It's as simple as that.

In the event of a tie, the chairman has the casting vote. However, not even these meetings are straightforward.

There's a "power struggle" going on between the smokers and non-smokers on the committee. Until one side gains "control," a compromise has been reached. For the first hour of the meeting, smoking is not allowed. For the second, it is.

Though, on the face of it, being managerless must be a big disadvantage, Stranraer secretary Jimmy Edmunds argues exactly the opposite.

"We are completely happy about the way things are going," he says. "And our money troubles seem to be behind us."

"As it is, we now have quite a healthy bank balance, and we sell more season-tickets than any other Scottish Second Division club."

Once the team is picked, it's then up to John Heap, a former player and now a fully qualified S.F.A. coach, to get them into shape for the game on Saturday. Though, once again, that's not quite as simple as it sounds.

Most of the players come from the West of Scotland and it would take a four-hour trip to report to Stair Park for training. So the players train around their own homes and meet at Stranraer on the day of the game.

Though for the moment, John and the Stranraer committee are content to try to take the club out of the Second Division, Stair Park has had its moment of European glory.

In the clubroom is a pennant presented by the Austrian side, Graz A.K., who played Stranraer during a British tour.

"The game cost us thousands," said secretary Edmunds. "We had to guarantee Graz more money than we could get in at the gates.

"That's why there's just the one pennant. We've never had a repeat."

JIMMY EDMUNDS — hard work behind the scenes

FLYING DOWN THE WING!

● **England star PETER BARNES** shows the style that can turn a defence inside out.

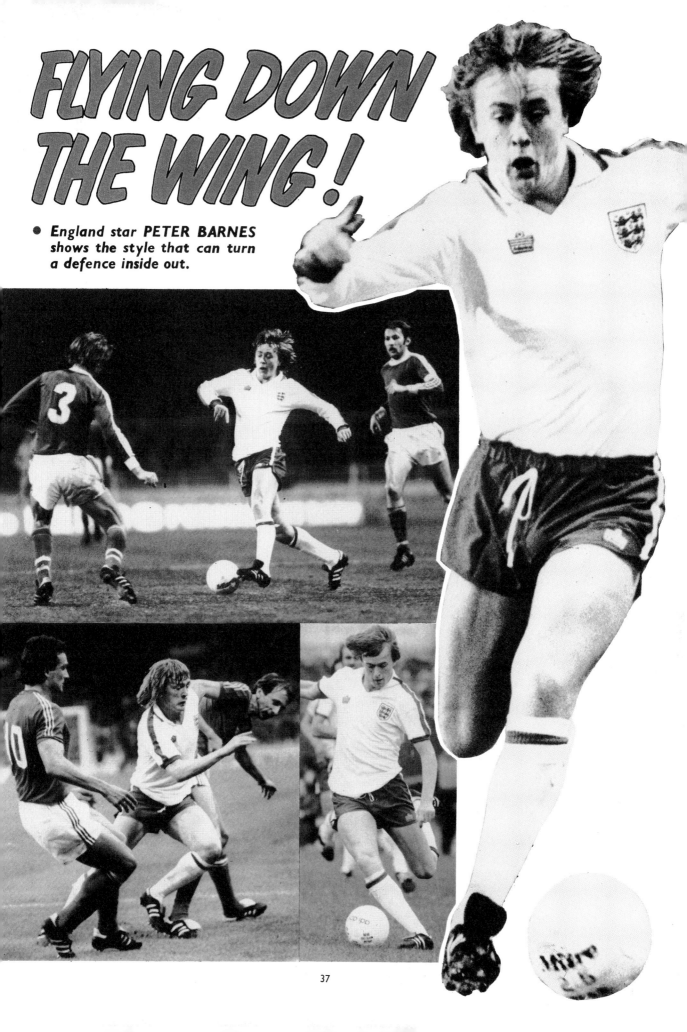

SILVER EAGLES
– JUST LOOK AT THEIR TROPHY ROOM

THE Eagles of Lisbon, the famous Benfica, are to extend their trophy room.

Which is hardly any wonder when you see how jam-packed it is.

But, though it is the club's most important function, and the one that makes most money, it's not only football that fills all the shelves.

The club has twenty-six other sections ranging from cycling and gymnastics to underwater fishing, rifle shooting, water polo, chess, badminton, basketball, tennis, boxing, motor racing and so much else.

Having won some four thousand national and international trophies, Benfica are the opposite of Britain's once-a-fortnight operators.

They have 50,000 members taking part in these many activities. All paying around £4 a head for it.

But the trophies that always matter are the European Cup, the Portuguese Championship and the National Cup.

The man responsible for producing a winning football section at the Stadium of Light, is English. He is John Mortimore, wing half with Chelsea. FA coach, former manager of Portsmouth, team boss of clubs in Greece before moving to Benfica in 1976 to the job previously held by former England International, Jimmy Hagan.

John Mortimore is one of the serious men of the game. An England amateur internationalist, he was schoolteacher before becoming a full-time professional with Chelsea in 1957.

Now 49, he is using his experience to try to restore

to Benfica the eminence they held in European football in the 60's. When the European Champions Cup seemed to be the personal property of Benfica, Real Madrid and Inter-Milan—until Celtic won in 1967, Manchester United in 1968—and the football changed.

"The trophy the whole of Lisbon wants to see back in the trophy room is the European Champions Cup," says John Mortimore. "That must always be the aim of any manager in Portugal. To win a place in Europe."

MAN IN THE BLACK GLOVES

A BIG problem for John Mortimore is that Portugal has now lost the African colonies of Angola and Mozambique. The Benfica of the 60's was built up on scouting in Africa. Producing players like Eusebio, Coluna, Aguas and Costa Pereira, who, in the current European transfer rating, would be in the one million pounds bracket.

Now it is laid down that only Portuguese nationals may play for the club, and Mortimore seeks to bring all his experience to bear in developing the natural ball-playing talents of the Portuguese players.

He has introduced a number of young players to the No. 1 team, who are now starting to do well in Europe.

As an ex-schoolteacher, John Mortimore has the ability to become at home in a Continental country. To get over difficulties by learning the language, for a start.

"Playing the game is the same the world over—it's just a question of making the best of the different temperaments," he says.

He also brought back the Portuguese mid-field star, Jose Alves, who had been playing with Salamanca in Spain. He is known as "the man in the black gloves"—because he always wears them when playing.

John Mortimore is making a hit at the sports complex that is the Estadio de Luz, which, apart from its 60,000 capacity, has a sports hall for 4,000, five gymnasia, medical centres, restaurants, parking facilities, space for at least half a dozen playing pitches, basket ball areas and tennis courts.

The club also runs a weekly newspaper—and adds dozens of trophies to the display every year—including cups won by the club's own choral group.

SHILTON - SAFE and SURE

Rated one of the world's top 'keepers, Nottingham Forest's PETER SHILTON knows he can only stay at the top by constant hard-work and practice. So, exhausting muscle-stretching sessions on the training ground are a must. All going to prove that practice makes perfect.

SWEENEY TODD —The name of the demon barber of bygone days is recalled in this present-day clash on the football field. On the right, GERRY SWEENEY, Bristol City on the left, COLIN TODD, Everton.

AIRBORNE

Coming out on top in this battle is Southampton's MALCOLM WALDRON. Forced to give second best is Aston Villa's ANDY GRAY.

ACTION

All in the air in this Aberdeen v. St Mirren clash are from l. to r.—ANDY DUNLOP, St Mirren, DOUG ROUGVIE, Aberdeen, JACKIE COPLAND, St Mirren and WILLIE MILLER, Aberdeen.

It's an all-out attack on the Coventry goal. Fighting it out, from left to right, are COLIN LEE, Spurs, JIM HOLTON, Coventry, JOHN LACY, Spurs and MICK FERGUSON, Coventry.

Climbing high is West Bromwich Albion's LAURIE CUNNINGHAM, as he soars above the Birmingham City defence.

ANDY GRAY
Aston Villa

STEVE COPPELL, Manchester United

Andy King

—football's one-man chat show

AROUND Merseyside I'm known as the "Chirpy Cockney." Always first with jokes and chat. Actually the nickname is well off beam . . .

For starters I'm not a Cockney. I'm not even a Londoner. I was born in a small village outside Luton. Before I started playing football professionally I'd been to London only a couple of times.

Then in 1976 I moved to Everton from Luton Town as a nineteen-year-old. Somehow I became saddled with the "Chirpy Cockney" tag.

I suppose I am a chatterer. But it's a bit of a cover. I'm not confident by nature. I get very nervous before a big game.

The chat calms me. But the reputation has grown so much I can't be quiet for even a minute. If I am someone's bound to say—"What's wrong? You must have a problem."

I suppose I have upset people by the way I joke around. But I never mean to hurt anybody.

I don't go in for the high life. I'm very attached to my family. At Luton I'd spent my free time walking around the local farms.

I was brought up in a village where everybody knew everyone else. I have so many aunts and uncles I can't even remember some of their names!

Though married and living on Merseyside I still see a great deal of my parents.

My dad travels to Everton matches with our London supporters club. My mum and uncle come to most games, too.

I suppose they support Andy King rather than Everton! Still it's great to know there is someone cheering for me whenever I play.

I was very homesick after moving North. I shared digs with an Irish youngster called Martin Murray. He was as bad as me. We'd just sit around looking at each other.

It was such a big change all round when I signed for Everton. After only 30 games for Luton the then Goodison boss, Billy Bingham, paid £35,000 to sign me. It was like stepping into a different world.

I'd come on as a Luton substitute once at Goodison and once at Anfield and been almost scared by the atmosphere.

Everton's training area is bigger than Luton's

DRESSING-ROOM LESSON I NEVER FORGOT

ground at Kenilworth Road! From the beginning I was in awe of what was happening around me.

I signed on Tuesday, played a reserve game Friday night, then was whisked away to a top hotel with the first team. They were preparing for the derby with Liverpool the next day.

DREAM COME TRUE

IT was a morning match as the Grand National was on at Aintree, just down the road. I watched the game then went with the other players to the National. It was like a dream come true.

But I soon learned the realities of playing for a top professional club. The next reserve game was at Coventry. We lost 6-5. I scored twice and felt I'd played well.

But, after the game, the reserve team manager, Ray Henderson, laid into us. The dressing-room doors were locked. No one was allowed in or out until he told us in no uncertain terms how unprofessional he thought we'd been.

That was when I first learned how important winning is to a club like Everton. The pressure was new to me, but I'm used to it now.

Two weeks later injuries to several first team players meant I was promoted from the reserves.

We beat Middlesbrough at home. Two days later we won at Derby and I scored twice.

I was a regular first-teamer the following season. I was surprised as I felt it would be some time after my transfer before I won a settled first team place.

Planning to get married, I bought a house and moved in on my own for a time before the wedding.

But not being too keen on cooking I wasn't having what you'd call a balanced diet and I found myself putting on a lot of weight.

By Christmas in my first full season I was the club's leading goalscorer. After the year turned I really tailed off.

Then I got married and settled to a routine again. My form levelled off and things got back to normal.

While I was on my own the Everton lads rallied round offering me hospitality to break my habit of going to the chip shop for all my meals.

Mick Lyons and his wife were tremendous. They often had me round for a meal. Mick and I became great friends.

Mick's the nicest bloke I've met in football. Nothing is too much trouble for him.

It was with Mick I began to visit kids in hospital. It's something I try to do as often as possible now.

Mind you, I'm a bit squeamish about hospitals. I faint at the sight of blood!

I remember playing at Old Trafford against Manchester United. Our defender, Terry Darracott, collided accidentally with striker Bob Latchford.

MICK LYONS — a great friend

Terry's tooth went through his lip and he collapsed. There was blood everywhere.

I fainted! Terry was OK but I had to be revived with smelling salts!

GOALS ARE A MUST

PEOPLE have said I'm a frustrated forward. I love scoring goals as much as a striker does.

I score a fair number from midfield but it is never enough. If I go a few games without scoring I become depressed.

In training it has been known for me to score nine out of ten in a five-a-side. I always have to be in the thick of the action.

I've played a few times up front in serious games, too, with mixed results.

Scoring should be a bonus for a midfield man but for me it's a must.

The goals have come pretty regularly so far. So has success since I moved from Luton to Everton.

People are saying I'm now worth ten times what the club paid for me. But I would have all sorts of regrets if I were sold.

DAVID MILLS. West Bromwich Albion splashed out £516,000 for his transfer from Middlesbrough.

BIG DE

BRIAN TALBOT, Arsenal's £425,000 buy from Ipswich.

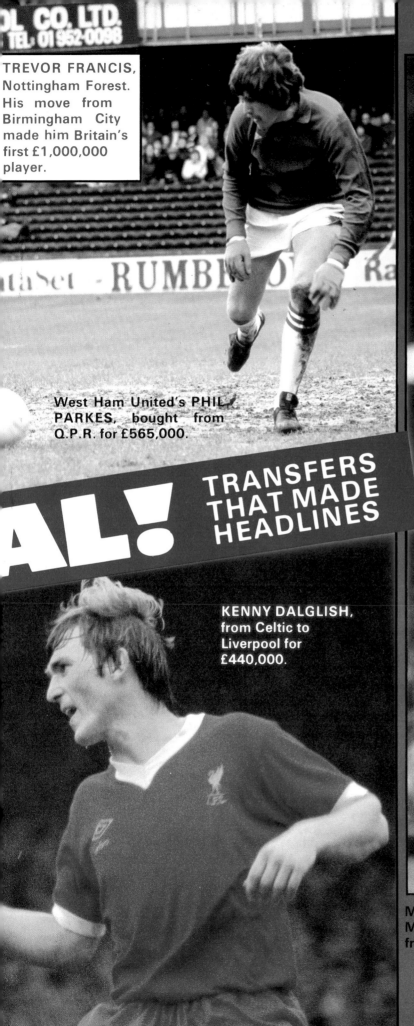

TREVOR FRANCIS, Nottingham Forest. His move from Birmingham City made him Britain's first £1,000,000 player.

West Ham United's PHIL PARKES, bought from Q.P.R. for £565,000.

TRANSFERS THAT MADE HEADLINES

KENNY DALGLISH, from Celtic to Liverpool for £440,000.

Manchester United's GORDON McQUEEN, a £450,000 transfer from Leeds United.

PAUL CLARK
Brighton

TOMMY HUTCHISON, Coventry City

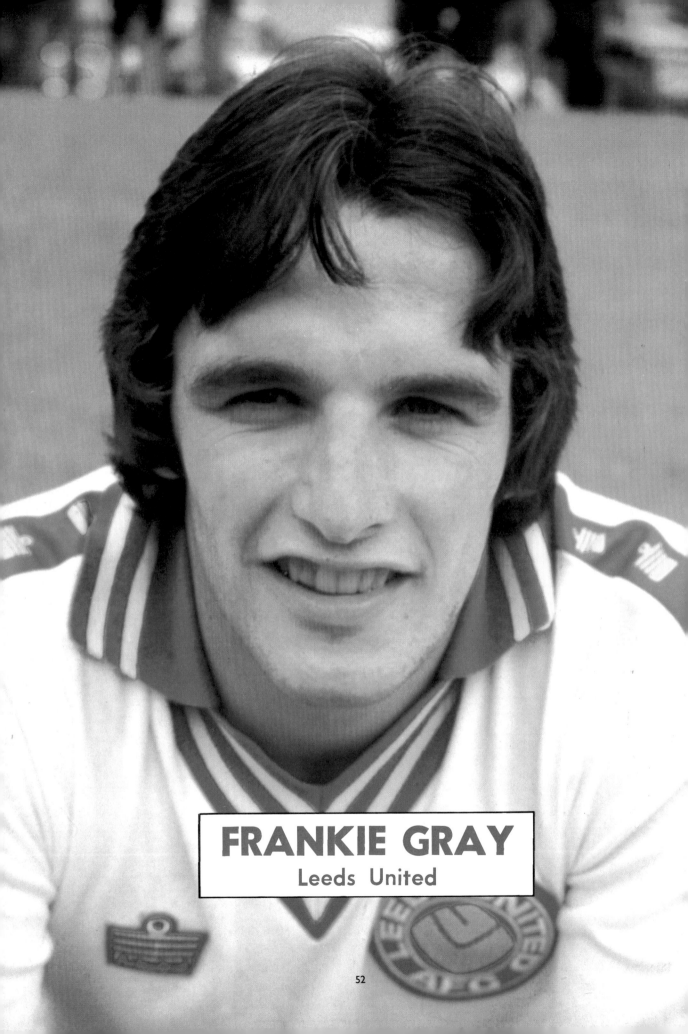

FRANKIE GRAY

Leeds United

52

GEORGE BERRY, Wolves

53

I'M A DRESSING-ROOM DREAMER

confesses
West Ham's
ALAN DEVONSHIRE

MANY top players have successfully bridged the gap between non-league and First Division football.

Cyrille Regis (West Brom), Gordon Hill (Derby) and Paul Mariner (Ipswich) are just three players missed by league clubs as youngsters and later signed from non-league clubs.

It happened to me too . . .

I was rejected by a league club as a schoolboy and took a job outside the game I so much wanted to be in.

So I have had some of the deep depression that comes from the feeling of having missed the boat—and the joy of suddenly getting the chance I thought had gone.

Everything happened quickly for me. Only a month after playing in the Isthmian League for Southall I was turning out for First Division West Ham.

To try to beat pre-match nerves and get my concentration together I turned to meditation.

Before a match the other West Ham players do exercises, warm up with a kick-about in the gym, or crack jokes to ease the tension.

Me—I'll be stretched out on a bench, eyes closed, flat on my back—meditating.

This way I find I can get into the right frame of mind for the game to come.

Of course, the other lads joke about it.

"Wake up, Brains, it's half-time," they said when I first started doing it.

I got the nickname " Brains " when I joined the club. Everybody at West Ham has a nickname.

Nobody calls me Alan.

Then, after turning up one day with a new hairstyle and moustache, I became George. Don't ask me why.

In the same way, David Cross is " Norman," Pat Holland " Monkey," and Paul Brush is, more obviously, " Basil."

The only one of my mates without a nickname is Trevor Brooking. He's just " Trev." He doesn't need a nickname to stand out. His ability does it all for him.

Since I got into the big team Trevor has helped my game. Telling me when to hold the ball and when to release it. How to find space and so on.

But all the players at Upton Park have been great to me. It could easily have been made awkward for a youngster from non-league football winning a first-team place so quickly. But I was accepted right away.

Now I am achieving my schoolboy dream of playing football for a living. The dream that, for a couple of years, was a nightmare.

A BITTER BLOW

AS a kid I was convinced I was going to turn professional after leaving school. I had trials with Crystal Palace when I was 14.

Then came the first blow. Their manager at the time, Bert Head, told me I was too small. He advised me to try again when I was 16.

HE'D CANTER A "SUPERSTARS" SHOW

Two years later I went back, signed as an amateur and played regularly for the junior teams.

I felt I was doing quite well. At 17, I was told I'd be offered professional terms.

The bottom dropped out of my world when Malcolm Allison took over as manager. I don't think he saw me play, but I was released as they trimmed the staff.

I was down in the dumps for months. I took a job in a factory in Southall. After a while I joined Southall, who play in the Isthmian League. Then West Ham came for me.

Signed on a Thursday, I played for the reserves on the Saturday. Three weeks later we had a Monday reserve game. The first team had a League Cup-tie against Queen's Park Rangers the following night.

I was told to report to the ground to take in the first-team atmosphere, though not listed in the squad for the match.

Forty-five minutes before kick-off, manager John Lyall asked me " Do you want to play? " Silly question . . .

I was nervous at the start and the game just seemed to pass me by. It was all so hectic. I didn't touch the ball in the opening ten minutes.

But as the game wore on I began to find my feet. At the end I was enjoying myself. We lost 2-0 but I felt I'd done pretty well.

I kept my place for another six weeks. And apart from a short break, I've stayed there ever since.

BONZO BEATS 'EM ALL

WITH West Ham, the accent is on skill rather than on the physical side. That will always be so.

After being relegated with the Second Division we also put extra emphasis on fitness.

When it comes to training runs one player beats everyone else. He's Billy Bonds. " Bonzo " to all of us. I reckon he could walk away with the T.V. " Superstars " contest.

If we have a training run Bill's finished and out of the bath before the next man comes in. He's like a machine. I thought I was pretty fit until I met Bonzo.

When I began full-time training it didn't come too hard. I simply fell asleep every afternoon once I got home!

It was harder to adjust to the quick thinking that First Division players must have. You have to react fast to keep up.

A regular goalscorer with Southall, it took me ages to get off the mark with West Ham. And I still feel I should be scoring more goals.

With my father, Les, I go over every game I play. Dad was a professional with Crystal Palace, Brentford and Chester. I recall chances I missed and we try to work out where I went wrong.

Dad keeps scrapbooks of my progress. He's as pleased as I am I've made the grade with West Ham.

He goes everywhere to watch me and will tell me if I haven't played well. I know I have to turn it on to impress him.

There's an amusing story in connection with my family. While I was in the Crystal Palace junior side, we had a game against Southend and found ourselves short of players.

They asked my elder brother Gordon to turn out. Some youth! He was about 23 at the time.

Gordon played centre-forward. Naturally the Southend youngsters gave him some odd looks. Especially when he scored two goals. A good job they didn't ask for his birth certificate!

I've rarely scored two goals in a match for West Ham, but I don't really worry about it. As long as the team is scoring it doesn't matter who gets the credit.

Football is a team game. One man can't do the lot.

That was something I had to learn at West Ham. I'd get the ball, and try to beat as many opponents as possible. And there always seemed to be one too many.

Trevor Brooking taught me the importance of awareness of team-mates.

" Always look around and make use of your support," was his message.

I'm still learning about the game. Being relegated was a blow, but in the long run, it's helped me develop confidence in my game away from the intense pressure of the First Division.

Now I hope to make the most of it by helping West Ham back to the top.

BILLY BONDS – Super fit

STRIKER STOPPER

BOB LATCHFORD
Leading the way for Everton

LARRY LLOYD
Strong man in defence for Nottingham Forest

JIMMY CASE, Liverpool

57

BEANFEAST

ARTHUR GRAHAM, Leeds United, speaks his mind — and shows the skills that make him a key man for club and country

FOR "BUMPER"*

I HAD seven happy years playing for Aberdeen before joining Leeds United.

I use the word happy because some folk in Scotland believe only trouble-makers ask for transfers to England.

They think footballers are somehow different from ordinary youngsters.

A player wants to further his career. When lads leave school and take a job, they don't expect to keep it for life. They hope to move on and up!

Nobody argues with that. But consider the case of the footballer.

He signs for a club at 15 and makes fine progress. Then, when he really makes the grade and hears top clubs are interested, it seems he is supposed to ignore all the talk.

That isn't expected of someone in any other job or profession.

The critics forget a footballer player is a professional. He wants to be as successful as possible. That is why so many Scottish clubs face transfer requests from their players.

When I was with Aberdeen I had no complaints at all about their treatment of me as I made progress into the Scotland international squad.

But there you hear of the wages being paid in England. You hear of the crowds and the atmosphere.

No player of ambition can turn his back on a chance of a big wage increase and a more exciting stage to work on.

That is the big difference between the Scottish and English leagues.

The standard of football in Scotland is higher than most people in England think.

Many of my former Aberdeen team mates, for instance, could step straight into the English First Division and give a good account of themselves.

But Scotland can't match up on crowds—except on the odd occasion. Most games lack the atmosphere of big grounds in England.

Atmosphere is tremendously important. If you run out in front of 5000 fans thinly spread on the terraces it gets you down.

> "Bumper"* was the nickname given Arthur at Aberdeen — after he'd been heard calling his training shoes "bumpers."

But if you come out of the tunnel in front of 50,000 cheering people you can feel the tingle of excitement.

That is what Leeds United have given me. I have improved my family's standard of living and I play in a league where every game is a big occasion.

At one stage I thought I would never get a chance in England.

I had been a year waiting for a transfer from Aberdeen and had heard rumours about clubs looking at me. But never was there a hint of a bid.

Meantime Aberdeen had transferred other players. I was beginning to think I was to be the one to miss out.

I was actually in Spain on holiday when I heard the news that Leeds United had made an offer. I couldn't get home quickly enough.

I had nothing against Aberdeen. But I felt I could improve my football career and way of life at Leeds. And that's how it has worked out.

The big battle at Elland Road these past two seasons has been to get back into Europe, from where the club was banned after the riots during the 1974 European Cup final against Bayern Munich.

Everybody who was with Leeds when they were in Europe keeps talking about the magic of a big European night.

It's been the ambition of all the younger players to help bring that extra spice back to the stadium.

Last season Leeds were hard hit by injuries. The manager asked me to have a go as a striker. I pack a pretty good shot but I'm not built for mixing with the big centre backs!

But one of the basic rules of playing a team game is that, while you may not fancy a particular job, there are times when you just have to get stuck in to help the team. And that I did.

We have a good spirit going again at Leeds. I'm sure it won't be long before we are back among the honours.

A sight that spells danger for any defence — **JOE JORDAN** Manchester United striker pounding for goal.

SO-HAPPY SAMMY

Full backs love to score!
So when Arsenal's
SAMMY NELSON
got his name on the
scoresheet against
Ipswich he had plenty
to shout about.

The camera tells a lie!

DAVE SWINDLEHURST, Crystal Palace, seems to be sitting on Fulham 'keeper, GERRY PEYTON.

When three balloons got caught up in the action, this Villa forward was left with a problem at his feet!

No, it's not a slap in the face for Nottingham Forest's ARCHIE GEMMILL. Team-mate JOHN ROBERTSON was just helping sort out a defensive "wall."

Flattened by Frank! This power-packed header by **FRANK STAPLETON**, Arsenal, certainly left its mark on the ball.

Looks as if **STAN BOWLES**, Q.P.R., is about to land one on referee **BRIAN DANIELS**. But Stan was only showing disappointment at being given off-side.

Is **ANDY KING**, Everton, putting his mark on Q.P.R.'s **RACHID HARKOUK**? No, it's the way the camera caught Mike's attempt to hurdle the prostrate Ranger.

GLAN LETHEREN, Chesterfield and Wales' Under-21 goalkeeper, is really putting the ball under pressure with this punch.

SKY-HIGH CYRILLE

West Brom's CYRILLE REGIS leaves no-one in any doubt how he feels about scoring against Manchester City. That explosive right foot shot gives Joe Corrigan not a chance.

JOHN DUNCAN, Derby County

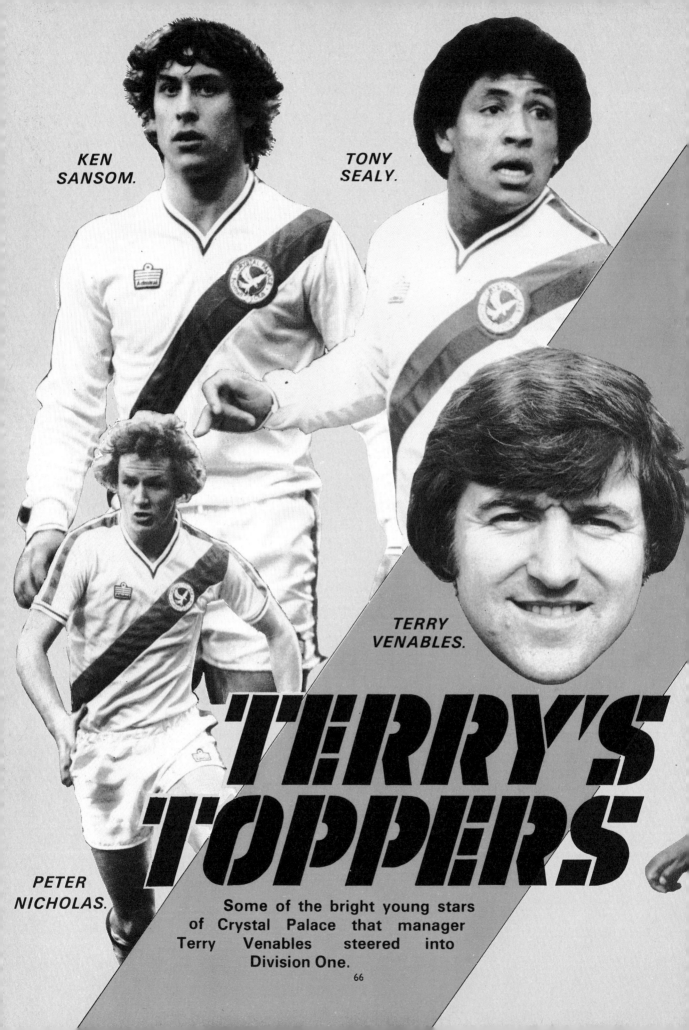

KEN SANSOM.

TONY SEALY.

TERRY VENABLES.

PETER NICHOLAS.

TERRY'S TOPPERS

Some of the bright young stars of Crystal Palace that manager Terry Venables steered into Division One.

JIM CANNON.

VINCE HILAIRE.

67

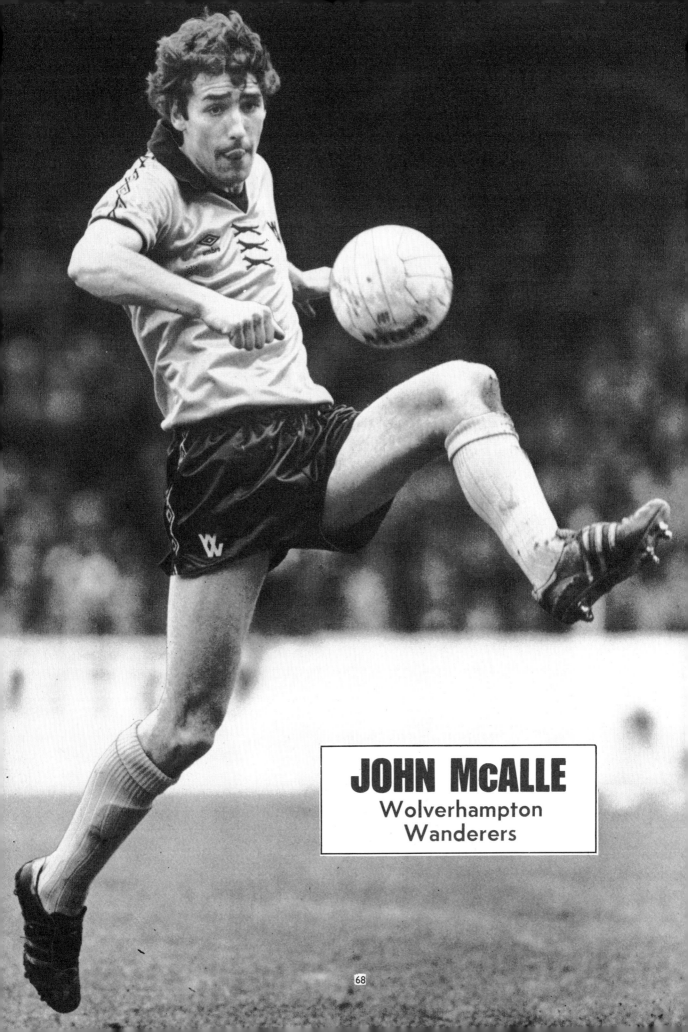

JOHN McALLE
Wolverhampton
Wanderers

CONCENTRATION — that's the name of the game for STEVE HARDWICK, Newcastle United keeper.

69

JOE LAID DOWN THE LAW AND PICKED UP THE LOLLY!

FINE DAYS

The Queen's Park Football Club, Limited

COMPANY REGISTERED IN SCOTLAND No. 5382

REGISTERED OFFICE
HAMPDEN PARK.
MOUNT FLORIDA.
GLASGOW. G42 9BA

FINES – SAT 18:11:78

J GILROY — £1 "speaking" to referee.

R EDGAR — 10p — swearing in dressing room

" — £1 — sent off

J M'ALOON — 50p — name-taken

I BALLANTYNE — 50p — name-taken.

D WOOD — 15p — dirty boots.

Please pay up as soon as possible ✱

J. Gilroy

FINES – SEASON 1978-79

1. Boots dirty and/ot not in box.	15p
2. TRAINING KIT not hung up.	15p
3. SWEARING in Dressing Rooms.	10p
4. " during training and/or game.	15p
5. " at COACH.	£5.
6. " at PRESIDENT.!!!	£500
7. Late for training.	10p
8. No phone call for absence.	10p
9. Missing training.	20p.
10. Disappearing "ad infinitum".!!!	£1000
11. Involved "verbally" with opponents referee; linesmen; spectators	25p.
12. Name taken	50p.
13. Sent off.	£1.
14. Not wearing club tie on MATCH DAY.	15p.
15. Shouting back at bench during game.	25p.
16. Arguing with Coach.	25p.
17. Arguing with Self.	50p.

✱ FINES CAN NOT BE PUT DOWN AS EXPENSES !!!

✱ ALL "DONATIONS" to end of season party.

QUEEN'S PARK, the only amateur club in British league football, has a system of FINES for players who step out of line.

What's more, the scheme has the approval of all the Hampden club's players! The idea came from former club coach, Joe Gilroy.

Joe wanted players to know what to expect if they slipped up, either in a game, or in training.

So he drew up a list of penalties which was pinned to the notice board in the dressing-room.

And what if someone should "forget" to pay his fine? Well, Joe thought about that as well. A bad-debt sheet was also prominently displayed.

Joe claimed it was a method of keeping the players on their toes. The money was used for an end-of-season celebration for all the staff.

JOE GILROY

BRIAN FLYNN
Leeds United

72

JOHN WARK

Ipswich Town

ALL in the GAME

Misprint in a paper in Antwerp. In an article about veterans, it said: " . . . one of the best players of Bristol City is Norman Hunter, who is 85-years-old."

Hibs goalkeeper Jim McArthur certainly found himself in the firing line during a derby game against Hearts. And it wasn't just from the Hearts forwards. After the game among the objects found behind his goal were two golf balls, 20 coins, cans, bottles . . . and a spanner!

Munich 1860 sweeper Ahmet Glavovic has set up something of a record. In the past two years he's been booked 36 times.

When West Bromwich Albion toured China last year they were astonished by the behaviour of the crowds at their games. Although 80,000 people were in the stadium the only sound was a ripple of polite applause when Albion scored.

If the crowd showed any signs of getting a bit noisier there would be a loudspeaker appeal for silence!

Watford's Ross Jenkins won three footballs last season—three that he scored hat-tricks with. At 6 ft. 4 in. Ross is the league's tallest striker and almost half his goal haul came from headers.

Norwich City had this wooden wall built, to help their players sharpen up free-kicks. Manager John Bond borrowed the idea from the South Americans.

George Berry, Wolves, was delighted when picked for Wales last season. But that was only one of five countries he was eligible to play for. They are—West Germany, where he was born, Jamaica, his father's birthplace, Scotland, England and Wales.

CHICKEN FEED

Transfer fees on the Italian island of Sardinia can be a bit out of the ordinary. One last season was no exception. The Nurri club transferred their star player Antonello Schirra to Suelli—for 1500 bales of hay.

Fulham midfielder John Margerrison has a name that's difficult to say and hard to spell. So when John was "booked" at a game, the ref had a problem getting the name right. The player eventually took the ref's notebook—and booked himself!

FULL MARKS TO THE FANS

Scottish Second Division side Meadowbank Thistle can't boast of large crowds. But they can claim to have one of the most enthusiastic fan clubs in the country. They're prepared to make a round trip of 700 miles to see a home game! Full marks to the London branch of the Meadowbank Thistle Supporters Club. Formed by two students, they have over 200 members.

An honorary member is television newscaster Reginald Bosanquet.

Joe Wark, captain of relegated Motherwell, didn't have much to smile about last season. But this pre-match encounter with comedian Andy Cameron raised a big laugh!

DAVE LANGAN
Derby County

PETER TAYLOR
Tottenham Hotspur

FUN AND GAMES WITH
OSSIE *and* RICCY

I WATCHED the 1978 World Cup Finals on television and admired the skills of Argentina's Osvaldo Ardiles.

I never imagined that, two months later, I would be sharing a hotel room with Osvaldo and his team mate Ricardo Villa!

It seemed unbelievable when Spurs splashed out over £700,000 to sign the two Argentinians.

Now it seems the most natural thing in the world. Ardiles and Villa are world-class players. Tottenham Hotspur is a world-class club. They go together like Rolls and Royce.

Naturally it wasn't easy at first for these two. It

OSSIE ARDILES
— skills to admire

always does take a new signing time to settle in. In my case at White Hart Lane it took the best part of a year.

For these men from Argentina it was much harder. Not only were they changing clubs, they were moving into a whole new way of life.

On our pre-season tour I shared a hotel room with Ossie and Riccy. They didn't speak much English. I didn't speak Spanish. But we got along famously.

It was funny at times. Ossie's pronunciation of Tottenham as "Tottingham" to rhyme with Nottingham still raises a laugh. And Riccy said once he thought England was "very barbarous". He didn't mean he thought we were all thugs. Apparently in Spanish it is a compliment.

There were times in training when the newcomers simply couldn't grasp the idea behind a particular routine and just fell about laughing. But they worked hard to learn our methods, and we did all we knew to understand their style. Gradually everything knitted together.

As I said it took me a long time to settle at White Hart Lane. Perhaps that had something to do with my £200,000 fee. Yet at one time, Spurs could have signed me for nothing.

As a youngster I had trials at the Spurs ground including a game in the junior side. But I was rejected for being one-footed.

Determined to make the grade in football, I went home and spent months working on my right foot. I didn't allow myself to kick at all with my left. In games with my pals I used only my right. Even though it meant all sorts of awkward moments.

I was determined to become as strong with my right foot as with my natural left. Now you'd be hard pressed to tell I was originally a "leftie."

Most of my time is spent on the right wing with Spurs. And I can cross a ball or shoot as effectively from either side.

Perhaps, had I been signed by Spurs at 15, I wouldn't have worked so hard nor done so well at the game. I certainly don't have any regrets.

I worked as a storekeeper for 18 months while playing as an amateur. When I became a professional with Southend United I knew I was well off.

PLANNING PAID OFF

S OUTHEND did a lot for me. But the man who was to make the biggest impact on my football was Malcolm Allison, when he bought me for Crystal Palace.

Malcolm made me into an internationalist. He gave me belief in my ability to reach the top. You see, I was always a player whose confidence came

on the Argentinian Connection

and went very easily. Up one minute, down the next.

Malcolm kept ramming home the point that I had the ability to be a great player. That if I believed in myself, I could do it.

In the space of 18 months everything came right for me. I won four Under-23 caps for England, scoring in every game. Then Crystal Palace began a fabulous F.A. Cup run to the semi-final, before losing to Southampton. And I won my first full England caps.

The Cup run was memorable.

Strangely, the game we lost in the semi-final was the only one we were confident of winning.

On the way to the semi we played Chelsea, Leeds and Sunderland—all away from home. We didn't expect to win any of these ties. But we did, thanks to the backroom planning of Malcolm and Terry Venables.

For each game they had a different tactical scheme. Each time it worked like a charm.

For the semi-final we felt we were the favourites, but the magic didn't come. We never found form.

At the same time I was progressing from the Under-23's to the full England team.

It was great playing for England. But I don't think I realised at the time just what it meant to be a part of the international squad. I suppose I took it for granted, because things were going so well for me at club level.

When out of the squad after joining Spurs, I realised I missed the involvement with the other players. It made me very keen to regain my place.

It was in the Under-23 squad I first linked up with Steve Perryman, now my best friend at Tottenham.

Steve played for the Under-23's as an " over-age " player, and we shared a room. He's a dedicated fellow. Since joining Spurs I have learned a tremendous amount from him.

SECOND TIME ROUND

MY first season at White Hart Lane was a disaster. I showed only patches of my best form. The team struggled, and, in the end, were relegated.

Steve was determined we should go straight back up. He set the mood for the team. His work as sweeper was a tremendous inspiration.

The spell in the Second Division gave everybody with Spurs a chance to regain their confidence. We started off scoring a lot of goals. It set us up for the season. Now we're back in the First Division—a much stronger side.

Spurs nearly missed signing me even second time round.

I spent an unhappy few months at Crystal Palace waiting for a club to make an offer matching Palace's valuation. From July to September I was available at £200,000, and I had an understanding with the club. If we didn't win promotion they would let me go.

Nobody seemed willing to pay the kind of money Palace wanted. As time dragged on, my own form suffered badly. After six weeks, fed up of the uncertainty,

I was ready to sign a new contract with Palace.

Then, just when I was about to tell Terry Venables I would stay, he told me Spurs had agreed a fee. I was on my way across London.

Apart from the confidence Malcolm and Terry Venables gave me, I took something else from Palace. Muscle was its name.

When I joined the club I was not particularly big-built. But I spent long afternoons doing weight-training. That did a lot for me.

It has given me the strength to win the ball in vital tackles. The power to knock over a cross at full stretch.

I feel strength in the tackle will let me drop back to mid-field in the future if I lose any pace.

It's useful to be able to play in more than one position these days. I also enjoy coaching and helping to run an amateur side in my spare time. This is good experience for any future job in the game.

But that's looking away ahead. My priority at the moment is to win medals with Spurs. With our Argentinian connection, I'm confident we can do it.

RICCY VILLA
— working hard

79

JOHN BIRD - in his true colours

John Bird sports the plain black and white of Newcastle United.

But off the field colour is the name of the game for John.

You see, not only does John run an art shop and gallery in his spare time—but he's also a bit of an artist himself.

Pictures with a seafaring theme are his speciality.

ERIC STEELE, Brighton

GEORGE BURLEY, Ipswich

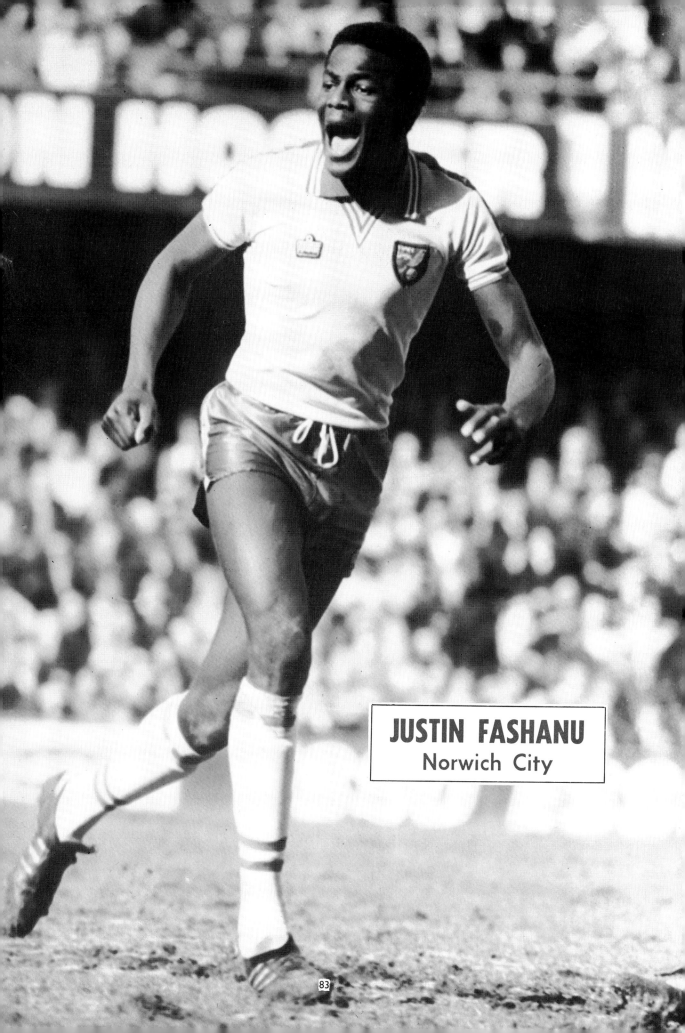

JUSTIN FASHANU
Norwich City

BIG GAME GET

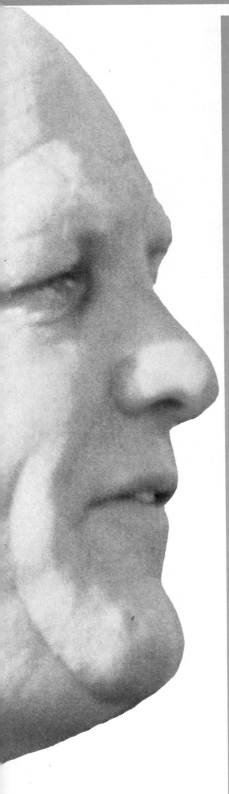

RAY KENNEDY
Liverpool

RAY WILKINS
Chelsea

TREVOR BROOKING
West Ham United

TOGETHER

KEVIN KEEGAN
S.V. Hamburg

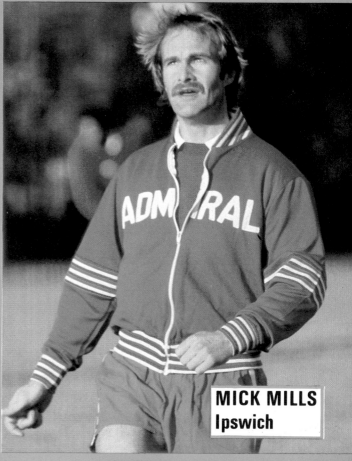

MICK MILLS
Ipswich

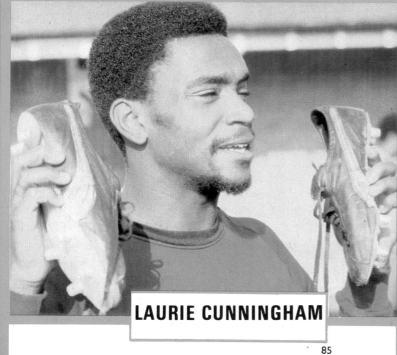

LAURIE CUNNINGHAM

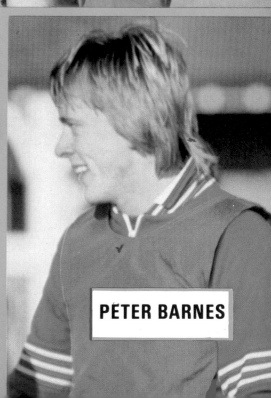

PETER BARNES

West Brom's Ron Atkinson talks about his black players

WEST BROMWICH ALBION have been hailed as the leaders of the " Black Revolution."

Many teams now include coloured players. But we are special. We have three of the best!

Cyrille Regis, Laurie Cunningham and Brendan Batson have become household names over the past couple of seasons. With good reason.

All three have the two assets all fans want to see—skill and breathtaking pace.

There have been times when some fans have mindlessly booed our coloured players. Like when we played Manchester United at Old Trafford last season.

At first, whenever Brendan, Laurie or Cyrille touched the ball a section of the crowd gave them stick. But none of the lads let the barracking affect them.

We played brilliantly as a team that day. The coloured boys were outstanding as we hammered United 5-3.

By the end the abuse had stopped. The Old Trafford fans, brought up on the skills of George Best, Denis Law, Bobby Charlton and the rest, realised they were seeing something very special.

Even in defeat many of the Old Trafford faithful told me they had just seen one of the best performances ever.

At The Hawthorns our black trio are nicknamed the " Three Degrees "—after the pop group who made a visit to meet the Albion players last season.

The one problem that troubles me is how good can our " Three Degrees " become?

Cyrille Regis—" Smokin' Joe," as he is known due to his resemblance to former world heavyweight champion Joe Frazier—is capable of scoring wonder goals.

I've seen him smash volleys into the net with both left and right foot. He doesn't have to trap the ball to set up a shot. He simply swings one of his powerful legs and whacks accurate drives from long range.

I admit there have been times when I've had a go at Cyrille, feeling he could become more involved in the game.

For instance, when we played Manchester City at Maine Road in a League game, I considered Cyrille wasn't putting himself about enough. I was very disappointed.

Then he collected the ball in our half and surged past four defenders. Reaching the City penalty area, he drew 'keeper Joe Corrigan and rammed the ball home.

It was a staggering goal. A goal I'm convinced only Cyrille Regis could have notched.

THREE OF THE BEST—
Albion's talented trio. From left to right — Laurie Cunningham, Brendan Batson, Cyrille Regis.

Afterwards the great Joe Mercer, formerly City manager and now a Coventry City director, acclaimed Cyrille's effort as the finest individual goal he had ever seen! A fitting tribute.

I just wish Joe had got a look at Cyrille's sprinting power on a pre-season tour of Scotland two summers ago.

Before playing Motherwell we agreed to enter three players in an eighty-yard sprint.

I nominated Cyrille, Laurie Cunningham and winger Willie Johnston (now with Vancouver Whitecaps). In the Motherwell line-up were Willie Pettigrew and Peter Marinello (now Fulham).

Willie Johnston was fastest from the start. After ten yards he was the clear leader. Then Laurie burst to the front.

Suddenly Cyrille turned on the power. He surged

past the lot of them, looking a magnificent athlete. He gave the impression he had simply changed up a gear to leave the rest standing!

When we actually played the football match that was no contest either. We hammered Motherwell 8-1.

After the game Roger Hynd, 'Well manager at the time, admitted to me his players had been scared by Cyrille's pre-match ' warm-up.' They didn't know how to stop him.

I have to keep reminding myself that less than three years ago Cyrille was an electrician who played for non-League Hayes.

His talent is incredible. With added bite and involvement he could make the England centre-forward berth his own.

THE BLACK PEARL

TALKING about talent leads me to the " Black Pearl "—Laurie Cunningham.

In my opinion Laurie is capable of becoming the greatest individual player since George Best. At times he does tricks with a ball you have to see to believe.

When I took over at The Hawthorns two years ago I understood Laurie had a " playboy " image. That he preferred night-clubs to football clubs!

I've found the tag to be completely wrong. He does like disco dancing, but he's a very quiet person off the field. And he takes his football very seriously.

I will never forget our U.E.F.A. Cup tie at Valencia last term. Laurie gave an incredible individual performance.

In the first minute his marker tried to hack him down. But that Spanish defender only managed to spur Laurie on.

No matter how tightly they tried to mark him, Laurie had the skill and speed to break clear. That night he displayed the extra commitment I asked from him.

Lack of commitment is one of the faults Laurie's critics point at. But I feel, over the past few months, he must have wiped out that particular slur.

Nobody could doubt Brendan Batson's determination. Over the past eighteen months he has established himself in the top flight. I feel his target now must be breaking into the England side.

International recognition was certainly a long way from my first meeting with Brendan, one of the players I inherited when taking over Cambridge United in 1974.

At the time he was operating in midfield, and we just didn't hit it off together. I didn't like his attitude. He thought I had a down on him.

During my first eighteen months at Cambridge I dropped Brendan, gave him several rollickings—and after sorting him out made him club skipper.

After a few months in charge of Albion I realised we needed a right-back. The club had been recommended to sign Peter Daniel from Hull City. He was rated in the £150,000 class.

CYRILLE REGIS — *a magnificent athlete*

But I wasn't keen to sign a player I knew nothing about. Peter joined Wolves and I went for Brendan.

Cambridge accepted £28,000 for him—and the most surprised person was Brendan. He never thought I'd go back for him.

Our coloured trio have been well-accepted by the other players at The Hawthorns. We even crack jokes about colour now.

Off the field I couldn't wish for three better ambassadors for the club. They are all immaculate in appearance and they conduct themselves well.

Black power is here to stay at The Hawthorns.

GARRY STANLEY
Chelsea

88

EYE ON THE BALL

"**T**HAT ball's gonna be mine!" is the message from ALLAN EVANS, Aston Villa (on the left) and PAUL McGEE, Q.P.R., in this no-holds-barred tussle.

OLÉ-

WITH twenty minutes left to play, Cranston Rovers were three goals down.

Sitting in the dug-out, I was beginning to tear my hair. Being one of the youngest managers in the league, I had plenty of hair to work on.

But Rovers looked like making me bald pretty soon.

My name's Bill Carter. I was Cranston's third manager so far that season. Friends had warned me against taking the job, but I was finishing my playing career. I wanted to get into management.

Second Division Cranston had seemed a good place to start. Now I was beginning to have my doubts. I could see what was wrong with the team. The difficulty was putting it right.

Our opponents were Eastwich. They were a middle-of-the-league club. Against us they looked like champions. Their winger raced down the line, then crossed. Their striker pounced, while Tony Oliver, our goalkeeper, stood on his line and watched.

"Get at him, Tony!" I croaked.

The striker hammered in a shot. Tony was still diving as the ball hit the back of the net.

I did some more hair-pulling.

The bench creaked as Mr Pearson settled his bulk down beside me. Here was one of the reasons why I had problems. Mr Pearson was chairman of Rovers. He ran a chain of supermarkets, and seemed to think this qualified him as a football expert.

"Not doing too well, Derek," said Mr Pearson.

"My name's Bill," I explained. "Derek was the last manager but one."

"Well, anyway, like I said, not doing too well," said Mr Pearson. "What we need is a new striker."

"There's nothing much wrong up front," I said. "Our defence needs tightening up."

"A striker's the answer," said

90

WHAT A GOALIE!

Mr Pearson, as if I hadn't spoken. "And I've got just the man for you, Derek. I've just had a telephone call from Mexico confirming the deal is on."

"Mexico?" I stuttered.

"Foreign players are the ones to go for these days," said Mr Pearson. "All the big clubs are doing it. I had a hot tip about a good one they've missed."

"Who gave you this tip?" I demanded.

"A chap who's living out there now. Reg Dobson. We were at school together."

"Reg Dobson? Is he in football? The name sounds familiar." Then it hit me, and I spluttered. "Reg Dobson! He's the bloke who left the country just one jump ahead of the police!"

"Er—yes," said Mr Pearson. "Reg does find it more convenient to live in Mexico at the moment. But he knows his football. He used to support Rovers."

A BIG SURPRISE

BLASTS from the referee's whistle signalled the end of the game. I gave a sigh of relief. At least we'd lost only 4-0.

"I think we'd better forget about this Mexican player, Mr Pearson," I said. "Excuse me, I want to talk to the lads."

"Hang on," said Mr Pearson. "I told you, I've clinched the deal. Here, look at this."

He pulled a scrap of paper from his pocket. It had been torn from a newspaper. There was a photograph of a swarthy, solemn-faced young fellow. Underneath was the name 'Pedro Martinez'.

"Reg sent me that cutting from a Mexican newspaper," said Mr Pearson. "It proves Martinez is a star out there."

"Pity there isn't more of the page, so we could read what the paper has to say about the lad," I said.

"Papers don't print big pictures of players unless they're stars," snapped Mr Pearson. "You leave everything to me. This new signing is going to surprise everybody."

He was right, too. We all got a surprise, including Mr Pearson.

At the beginning of the next week, I had the lads out on the pitch for a training session. It didn't make me feel any better when I shot at goal, and Tony let it run between his legs.

"My father wants me to join him in his plumbing business, boss," said Tony. "I'm thinking of taking up the offer."

"It might be a good idea, Tony," I agreed.

It was then Mr Pearson marched out on to the pitch. With him was a dark young fellow huddled in an overcoat.

SHORT STORY

"Here he is, Bill," said Mr Pearson, getting my name right for once. "Pedro Martinez! I've just met him off the plane. He doesn't speak much English."

Pedro looked round, and frowned.

"The bull," he said. "Where the bull?"

"Eh?" I said. "Oh, you mean the ball." I picked one up.

I mimed a kick, and tossed the ball to him. Pedro took a swing at it, missed, and fell flat on his back.

"Maybe he'd better get changed, then I can see how he shapes," I suggested.

"Good idea," nodded Mr Pearson. "He's brought his gear with him. It's in the dressing-room."

I waved my arms at Pedro, imitating a man undressing. He stared at me, then nodded.

"Si, si!" he said.

As he hurried away towards the dressing-rooms, I scratched my head.

"We'll have to try to find somebody who speaks Spanish," I said. "The lad seems all at sea. Looks as if he's just been dropped down on Mars. ."

SWINDLED!

PEDRO came marching back again. Mr Pearson looked at him and gasped. I was doing a bit of goggling myself. Pedro wore a tricorn hat, an embroidered jacket, silk breeches and stockings, and buckled shoes. He stopped and stood proudly before us. Sweeping off his hat, he gave a low bow.

The other players gathered round, their eyes bulging.

"Cor!" said Tony Oliver.

"That—that's a suit of lights!" I stuttered. "The outfit worn by a bullfighter!" I pointed at Pedro. "Matador?" I said.

A broad smile appeared over Pedro's face, and he nodded vigorously.

"Si, si!" he beamed. He lowered his head, and put up his hands like horns.

"Ole! Toro!" he shouted.

"Your friend Reg Dobson has conned us, Mr Pearson," I said. "And he's made a mug out of Pedro as well. We thought we were getting a striker. Pedro thinks he's been sent here to fight bulls. And Dobson is skipping away with the transfer fee!"

Matt Morris, our left back, and the team joker, had been studying Pedro with interest.

"What a carry-on!" said Matt. "But it's a great outfit!" He grabbed Pedro's hat and clapped it on his own head. "How do I look?"

Pedro muttered something in Spanish and jumped forward. Matt grinned and slung the hat towards Tony.

"Catch!" he shouted.

Pedro made a sideways leap, thrust out a hand and caught the hat. I stared at him. Matt whistled.

PEDRO PUTS PAID TO CITY

"Some catch!" he said.

"Too true!" I agreed. "I wonder if he could do it again?"

Pedro was cramming his hat back on his head. I picked up a football and signalled I wanted him to catch it.

I hurled the ball at Pedro. He did a quick wiggle, and the ball shot past him. I picked it up and threw it again. Pedro swayed aside again. But this time he thrust out a hand, grabbed the ball, and hurled it away.

I clapped Pedro on the shoulder. "It was just a test, chum. Nobody's trying to take the mickey. Come on, we'll find you some proper gear. Maybe you won't be going home just yet."

Leading Pedro to the dressing-room, I called to the others.

"Get hold of an interpreter! Try the university, the Spanish Tourist Office, anybody!"

In the dressing-room, I gave Pedro a training strip and tracksuit. He was getting more confused by the minute, but I kept on at him. He shrugged and changed into the gear.

Leading Pedro out, I put him between the posts and made signs that I wanted him to keep goal. He'd seen football played in Mexico, of course, and quickly caught on. He shrugged, and crouched on the line.

I banged a shot high to his left, Pedro jumped effortlessly across and touched the ball over the bar. Matt hit a ball to the right. Pedro seemed to change direction without touching the ground, and tipped the ball round the post. All the lads rained in shots. Pedro hurled himself round the goal as if all the bulls in Mexico were after him. Not a shot got past.

Then up came Mr Pearson with a brisk young fellow who introduced himself as a lecturer in Spanish at the university. I explained the situation, and he and Pedro started a natter.

"I want him to play in goal for us," I said. "Ask him if he's willing."

Another natter, then Pedro looked at me. He nodded his head vigorously, and beamed.

"Si, si!" he said.

"Great!" I said, "Well, I'm not sure how much a bullfighter knows about football, so perhaps you'll help me give him a bit of coaching."

It was soon obvious that Pedro had been too busy bullfighting to learn much about football, but he was a bright lad. He soon caught on to what was expected of him.

Alan Yates, our regular striker, was looking relieved.

"Lucky for me he's not a striker, boss," he said. "I was expecting to be out."

"You're very much in, Alan," I said. "With the defence tighter, the pressure will be off our front men. You can start scoring."

IT'S THE REF.! HE'S GOT WRITER'S CRAMP!

"MAGIC!"

MY brave words were tested in our next home game, against Dancaster City. I hadn't released any details about Pedro, and a big crowd had gathered to watch our new mystery star. They gave Pedro a cheer as he trotted to his goal.

He got another cheer a minute later. The City started off with a rush, and their striker tried a quick one. Pedro bounded across the goal, collected the ball calmly, and flung it out.

After that, the traffic began to flow the other way. Knowing there was such a safe pair of hands behind them, our defence settled down, playing with real confidence. They stopped a City attack, pushed the ball up front, and we were away. Alan ran on to a pass, swerved round a defender, and hammered home a shot.

City came back. They broke through once or twice, but Pedro was there. He bounced about his goal as if he had springs in his boots. He plucked shots out of the air, dived to smother them on the ground.

We broke away again, and Alan popped his second one in. City tried to get back into the game. Pedro rose above a crowd of players in the goal mouth, and pulled the ball down.

Pedro hurled the ball to Matt. The Rovers passed the ball from man to man down the field in a fast attack that had the crowd yelling. Alan got his head to the ball. In it went for his hat-trick.

With a 3—0 victory to us, the game ended. I met the lads coming off, and slapped Pedro on the back.

"Magic!" I said. "You've got a great future in the game, Pedro. Unless you want to go back to bullfighting."

"Not blooming likely!" he said. "Ball hurt less than bull!"

My day was complete when the directors sent for me. I entered the board room and found an argument going on.

"Well, it turned out all right in the end!" Mr Pearson was protesting.

"Only thanks to our manager!" said Mr Harvey, the senior director. "You bought a striker who turned out to be a bullfighter!"

He turned to me. "Bill, we're voting Mr Pearson out of the chair. I shall be chairman, but I shan't interfere. The running of the team is your responsibility."

"There's only one answer to that, gents," I said. "Ole!"

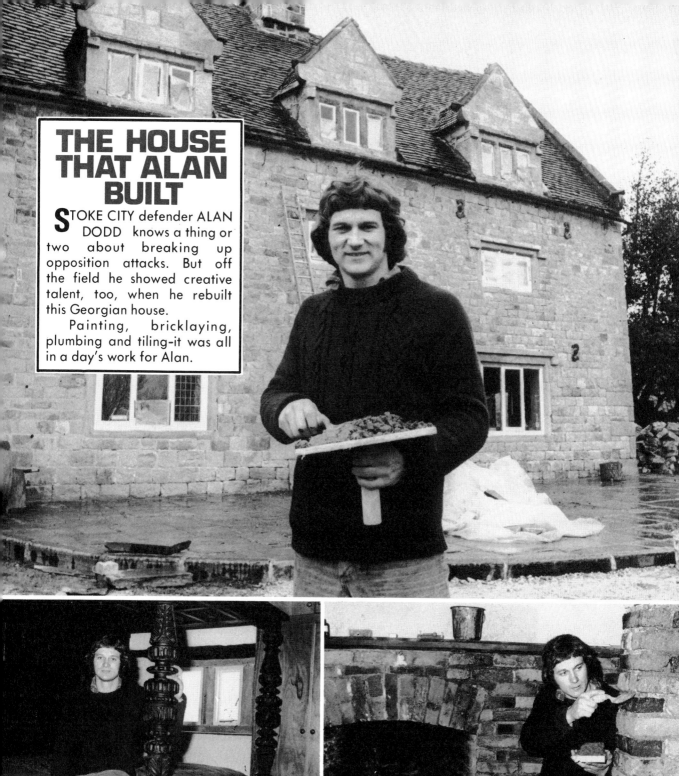

THE HOUSE THAT ALAN BUILT

STOKE CITY defender ALAN DODD knows a thing or two about breaking up opposition attacks. But off the field he showed creative talent, too, when he rebuilt this Georgian house.

Painting, bricklaying, plumbing and tiling-it was all in a day's work for Alan.

Alan's pride and joy —his four poster bed.

Alan applies the finishing touch to some interior stonework.

PELE

CRUYFF

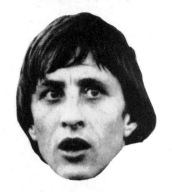

BECKENBAUER

STEVE'S STUNNING SOUVENIRS

FIVE hours was all I was given to make the biggest decision of my career.

To stay in England and battle away in Aston Villa's reserves, or join New York Cosmos, the United States' top soccer side.

It may look an easy choice. But I'd been married just a month, and hadn't a clue what awaited me 3,000 miles away.

It was a heart-searching decision. And five hours isn't long!

I rushed home from Villa Park to my wife at our house in Birmingham. After weighing up everything we decided on the Cosmos. That was in 1977.

How right we were. Going to America was the best move I ever made.

Yet only weeks before Cosmos offered me terms, my football future looked far from bright.

I'm sure I would now be a run of the mill Second or even Third Division player had I not moved!

I had been with Aston Villa since I was an eleven-year-old! Playing for their nursery side, I was on schoolboy forms.

I signed up as an apprentice at 16, and was a full professional at 17. After my first game for Villa I had to have a cartilage operation. But I made a good recovery and was soon back in the side.

The last game I played for Villa was the League Cup quarter final tie at Villa Park against Millwall. We won 2-0, Villa eventually beating Everton at the third attempt to win the trophy.

I was told I had played well against Millwall by our manager, Ron Saunders. But, after that match, I never got another look in.

Ron Saunders is a good manager. Unfortunately, we never saw eye to eye. I didn't want to leave Villa because they were my boyhood team. But I could see I had to move on if I was to better myself.

Coventry's
STEVE HUNT
on
Soccer American Style

I wouldn't have joined any other side in the United States but Cosmos.

I felt they must have a lot going for them if they could attract the greatest footballer in the world, Pele.

However, when I first got over there, the crowds were low and the standard of play poor

With only a small flat in New York, my wife and I were soon very homesick. But I decided to stick it out. And, gradually, we got used to the set-up and settled down.

By the end of my first season Cosmos crowds had risen to 70,000. I had become one of the crowds' favourites—and that alongside players like Pele and Franz Beckenbauer. We moved into a lovely apartment looking out to the New York skyline. Things looked good!

Pele and Beckenbauer really amazed me. I thought they wouldn't have much time to spend with the lesser-known players. I was completely wrong. They were always willing to stop behind after training and help out with any problem!

After a game Pele would stay until he had signed every autograph for the waiting youngsters.

Unasked, he would take me to one side and go into some aspect of my game.

When I was in England I was often booked for stupid things. I saw Pele coming in for a lot of harsh treatment, too. But he would always walk away from trouble. From him I learned how to keep a cool head.

The game in America is improving fast, of course. I have been lucky all along to be playing with the best team out there. By the time I had left, the North American Soccer League had become very strong.

The more open, less-defensive game suited me. Then I liked their 35-yard line which created the only area in which you can be offside.

Their no-draws idea with sudden death kick-ins to decide makes for more excitement, too.

"WHY ON EARTH DID I COME BACK?"

It's still very much a family game in the States. Fans arrive hours before a match starts. Fairs and barbecues are held in stadium car parks.

The razzamatazz doesn't stop, either, when the game begins. There are the cheerleaders, dancing on the sidelines, pianos playing and sometimes the teams are brought on to the pitch on siren-sounding fire engines.

Then there are the fantastic score-boards, flashing out action replay pictures of goals and comments like "Did you see that?" and "What a goal!"

I know what the big question is in all your minds... "Why on earth did I come back?"

When I signed for Cosmos I always said I wanted to return to England. I simply wanted to prove myself over here, always having had belief in my own ability. You see, I had never turned it on back home.

So, as soon as I heard Coventry City were interested in me, I shot back.

I have a lot of re-minders of my time in USA. For a start Cosmos won the Soccerbowl in both my seasons with them. That is the big one on the American soccer calendar.

There were no medals for winning. Instead we got gold rings with a big stone in the centre. One is par-ticularly special to me because I won it in Pele's last season. The ring is engraved with his auto-graph.

Twice I won a ball for scoring a hat-trick. Also I have huge scrapbooks crammed with photo-graphs given to me by press photographers.

But my most prized mementoes are three Cosmos shirts worn by Pele, Beckenbauer and Johan Cruyff. The one I missed was my schoolboy hero, George Best.

I look through my scrap-books and other mementoes. Then think where I could have been now if I hadn't gone to America.

To do so was the best decision I've ever made.

STEVE HUNT —
the Soccerbowl in his hands

CUP FINAL FEVER

The drama and tension of a Wembley Cup Final are mirrored in the faces of Arsenal's WILLIE YOUNG (left) and Manchester United's JOE JORDAN.

JIM McDONAGH
Bolton Wanderers

97

PLAYER-MANAGER TELLS HIS COACH—
GIVE ME STICK

I MADE a vow the day I became player-manager of Stockport County.

It was that I would stop playing the minute club coach Trevor Porteous or any of the team felt I was over the hill.

In my time with Swindon Town, Manchester City, Burnley, Blackpool, Stockport and England, I've always enjoyed my football.

I no longer have the pace that won me eight England caps. Now I use my head and let the younger lads do the running.

But I believe I can do a good job in the Fourth Division. I'm pleased to say my team-mates seem to agree.

Being a player-boss does create some problems though.

I don't train as hard as I did in my Maine Road days. I would struggle on a Saturday if I forced myself through gruelling mid-week sessions.

But I supervise training sessions for the rest of

Stockport's MIKE SUMMERBEE says his piece.

the lads. And I tell them sessions like these helped me reach the top.

I learnt a lot from the managers and coaches I played under.

Malcolm Allison, at Manchester City, and Jimmy Adamson, at Burnley, were probably the two best tacticians.

Adamson was a brilliant coach, with a superb insight into the game.

"Big Mal" brought the best out of players. At half-time those who were doing well were brought to earth with a bit of criticism. At the same time he boosted lads who were struggling.

A difficult job for any manager is to stop players getting bored during months of training. Malcolm knew how . . .

He varied training in a way that kept everyone on their toes. Now I copy many of his ideas.

Both Adamson and Allison could really get players buzzing for them.

Yet I'll let you into a secret. In the dressing-room before a match you couldn't meet two more different people.

Allison never shuts up. He has advice for everyone. He sends his team out bubbling with confidence.

Adamson hardly speaks before a game. He has a team talk earlier in the day, then just asks his men to concentrate on their task.

NO SPECIAL FAVOURS

THE half-time team talk is a problem for me. Out on the park, involved in the game, it's hard to analyse how we're doing.

So at the break I let Trevor Porteous do the

● JIMMY ADAMSON — brilliant coach

"ON THE PITCH WE ARE ALL EQUAL"

talking. I've also told him to give me " stick " if I'm not doing my job in the team.

If I make a mistake during the game I expect to hear about it. I ask for no special favours as boss. On the pitch we are all equal.

Discipline is a word folk keep mentioning to me.

I don't have the best disciplinary record in the business. So how do I deal with players who step out of line on the park?

I've never fined any lad who gets stuck in. If he's booked for a foul when he's challenging for the ball I have no complaints. But I would fine him for pulling out of a tackle!

I don't feel the Stockport lads are paid enough to start docking their wages every time they are shown the yellow card.

I don't condone dissent. But when a Fourth Division man is suspended he misses his appearance money and his bonuses. That seems sufficient punishment to me.

I treat players with respect. And I tell them they won't find a better boss to play for!

As a player-manager it would be very easy for football to completely occupy my mind. But I don't allow that to happen.

I'm determined to spend time with my family. And I've had a business interest outside football for ten years.

THE LAUNCHING PAD

TO give time to all these commitments isn't easy. I'm up at seven o'clock every morning and take my two children to school.

I'm behind the manager's desk at Edgeley Park by 8.45 a.m. I'll take the training session and deal with any correspondence.

Then, in the afternoon, I visit the shirt-making firm I own in Manchester. Normally I won't arrive home until at least 7 p.m. A twelve-hour working day is quite normal.

When I accepted the manager's job I said I'd do it my way. I've been pleased how well things have gone.

I reckon Stockport one of the best footballing sides in Division Four. But results are important. If we miss promotion we may be branded as failures.

Still our style has brought distinction to Edgeley Park. And probably put us on the right footing for success in the future.

Our narrow League Cup defeat by Manchester United last season won us respect. We deserved to beat them. All the lads were disappointed to go down 3—2 at Old Trafford.

That, then, was the launching pad. We have a fine ground and training facilities as good as any in the country. I'm happy to be player-manager of Stockport County.

● MALCOLM ALLISON — tops for tactics

ALEX MACDONALD, Rangers.

Left to right:-
GEORGE McCLUSKEY, Celtic.
PETER McCLOY, Rangers.
ROY AITKEN, Celtic.

TOMMY McLEAN, Rangers.

100

FIRM

For razor-sharp rivalry and electric atmosphere, the Rangers v. Celtic clashes are second-to-none. Here's a line up of players from both these clubs.

Left to right:-
JOHNNY DOYLE,
Celtic.
ALLY DAWSON,
Rangers.

PETER LATCHFORD, Celtic.

DANNY McGRAIN, Celtic.

Left to right:-
ALLY DAWSON,
Rangers.
GEORGE McCLUSKEY,
Celtic.
JO EDVALDSSON,
Celtic.
SANDY JARDINE,
Rangers.
COLIN JACKSON,
Rangers.

JOE ROYLE
Bristol City

GEORGE WOOD
Everton

MALCOLM PAGE
Birmingham City and Wales

DEREK STATHAM
West Bromwich Albion

105

AXED

ARSENAL'S
Frank Stapleton
EXPLAINS WHY

A STRIKER in the First Division has it tough. Hard tackling, relentless defenders see to that!

It's a supreme test of skill, too. Because teams pack their defences and give opponents little time or space.

That's why I find it so satisfying playing centre-forward for Arsenal. Every game is a challenge and that's the way I like it.

I'm proud to be able to take the punishment handed out by defences without retaliating.

My attitude is that if I lose my head when a player gives me a rough ride, then he knows he's getting on top.

Football is a man's game, with a lot of physical contact. I try to turn that to my advantage.

My childhood in Dublin has helped me accept the physical side of league football.

At school we played only the Gaelic version of the game and some hurling. In Gaelic football there are more hard knocks than in soccer. So, from an early age, I was used to getting knocked about.

I enjoyed sport at school, but I preferred to play soccer on Sundays for a boys' club.

Football on television has influenced me greatly. As a school kid I watched Manchester United a lot on the screen. I became a fan of Bobby Charlton, George Best, Denis Law and the others.

When United offered me a week's trial I could hardly believe it. I was perhaps a little overawed by the surroundings at Old Trafford, but was more impressed with Arsenal.

I went to Highbury for only two days. They were even more enjoyable than the week at Manchester United, and another I spent with Wolves.

I knew Arsenal were the club for me. So I signed as an apprentice.

HARD WORK

I STILL do a lot of TV football watching. Always on the look-out for new ideas.

I'm sure most players in Britain gain from studying foreign players who have come into the league. They seem to have more ball skill than us. In return perhaps they can learn from our fitness and commitment.

When I first signed for Arsenal I was better at heading the ball than controlling it. I had to work hard to become a better all-round player.

I'll always remember the marathon coaching sessions with the youth team. Doing the same drills time after time.

I know coaches sometimes lost their temper with me because I couldn't get it right. I resented them making me do things again and again. And I'd crawl home to fall asleep, exhausted.

But I always believed I would master the skills. I never lost faith in my ability. Every day I was there ready for more work. Eventually things began to come right. But I still work hard at the game. I'm not the kind for whom things come easily.

My ability in the air was developed playing in a Dublin street. It was too narrow for a proper game, so we took turns to cross the ball for the others to head at goal.

Hours of that taught me how to time my jumps to win the ball. Now I don't have to think about it too much. I can concentrate on trying to pick my spot. Aiming for the most difficult place for the 'keeper to reach.

WEMBLEY NIGHTMARE

SOME of my best football moments have been with the Eire international squad.

The morale is fantastic. They are a fine, happy crowd. We have a lot of fun.

Team manager Johnny Giles has done a marvellous job with Eire. I say that, even though he handed me one of my biggest disappointments last season.

For months I had looked forward to the European Championship tie against England in Dublin. On the eve of the match Johnny Giles told me he was leaving me out of the team.

Perhaps I had started the season a bit sluggishly. But being omitted was just the gee-up I needed. I made up my mind I would fight my way back into the side. I'd never give John any reason to leave me out again. His decision spurred me into finding the form that helped Arsenal win the F.A. Cup.

Our defeat by Ipswich in the '78 final will always be a nightmare for me—and everyone else at Highbury. Ipswich deserve credit for playing well. But we didn't do ourselves justice at Wembley. I don't think we strung two passes together all afternoon. Yet the longer the game lasted the more I believed we were going to win!

I've played in several matches in which one team has all the game but cannot score. Then the other side snatches a goal.

I could see us landing the F.A. Cup that way, particularly when Ipswich hit the woodwork three times. I was almost convinced we would go on to win a victory we didn't deserve. Until Roger Osborne finally got the goal that beat us.

The man I felt sorry for was Malcolm Macdonald. It was his third losing final at Wembley. Malcolm had done so much to help me settle into the Arsenal side.

When I first won a place he talked to me about goalscoring. How to get a shot in early. How to be in the right place at the right time and so on.

Malcolm was Arsenal's main target man. The player our midfield men and defenders looked for.

But when Malcolm dropped out after his cartilage operations, main scoring responsibility fell on me. I got more of the ball, and enjoyed the pressure.

Also I started to work up a good understanding with Alan Sunderland, who has the kind of sharpness I'm trying to add to my game. Speed off the mark can mean the difference between scoring or being blocked out. My pace is OK once I get into my stride, but I'm trying to sharpen up my quickness off the mark.

All the time I'm aiming to become an all round player and not just a goalscorer. Some strikers live for goals. They are on top of the world when scoring, and really down when the ball is not going in the net.

I enjoy scoring. But goals are not all the game is about to me. I wouldn't worry over not scoring if the team was successful and I was playing my part. My enjoyment is in playing well as part of the team.

I'd rather score five goals a season in a successful team than 30 in a mid-table side.

I'm still only 23. In the future I hope for real success with Eire at World Cup and European Championship level—and with Arsenal, of course.

I'll keep working at it . . .

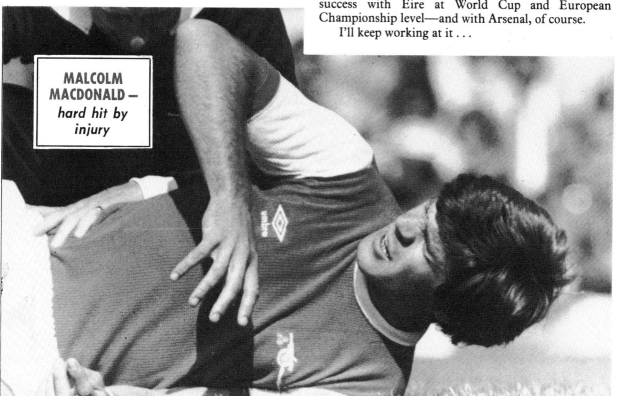

MALCOLM MACDONALD — *hard hit by injury*

DEAD-EYE

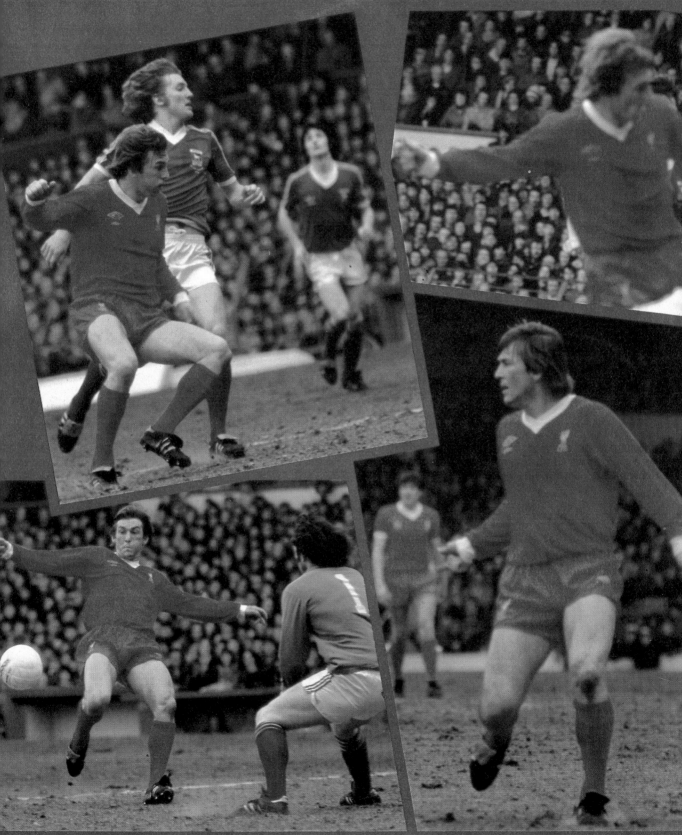

DALGLISH!

Liverpool and Scotland's goal grabber in action. And that means danger for any defence. The sure shot striker's formidable scoring record has made him a football superstar.

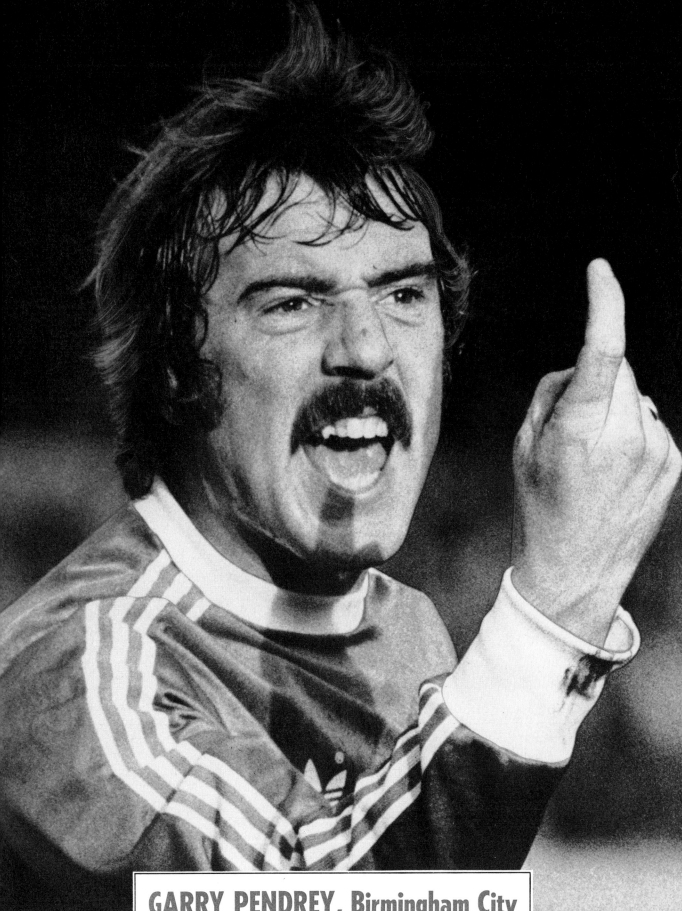

GARRY PENDREY, Birmingham City

BIG HEAD

THE TAG I HAD TO GET RID OF!

FOR years my dream was to play First Division football.

But when I moved to Manchester City last season I wondered if it was going to go wrong.

The problem was that I was quoted in the papers as saying I had signed for City to become a star. Pretty cocky coming from someone who had just left Third Division Plymouth Argyle!

Some City players obviously thought so, too. For a few games I hardly got a pass from some of them.

Happily that is all sorted out now. What I had said was I wanted to be part of a successful City team. If that happened then I would be one of the stars. That is every player's ambition.

When the City team realised I was no big-head I was accepted.

MANCHESTER CITY'S
BARRY SILKMAN
TELLS HIS STORY

I have enjoyed my move to Manchester. It gave me another chance to work with Malcolm Allison. Malcolm is one of the best coaches in the game. He refuses to judge a player by his reputation. He takes a long hard look at you and then makes up his mind.

When I was at Plymouth, Malcolm was in charge for a spell. He told me I had enough skill to play in the First Division. He also showed me I was wasting my time trying to play in one fixed position.

I was given a free role to go anywhere on the pitch where I felt I could help the team.

It gave me a whole new approach to football. I began to appreciate what it meant to be a team player rather than an individual.

Obviously Malcolm reckoned I had improved.

When he took over as Manchester City coach, he came back to sign me from Plymouth.

There were plenty of stories at the time about unrest in the City dressing-room. Like so many football rumours they were a long way from the truth.

There were obviously some players like Dave Watson, Asa Hartford and Peter Barnes, who felt a move would be good for their careers.

But whatever their personal problems they didn't take them out on to the pitch. The City players are all top professionals. On the field they always gave 100%.

The club, too, have shown they are determined to put Manchester City back on top. Their efforts to sign Mike Flanagan from Charlton Athletic for £750,000 proved that!

Last season was a big disappointment for everyone at Maine Road. City were rated to do well in the League—but it didn't work out like that. Then came that shattering cup defeat by Shrewsbury. It only made matters worse when rivals Manchester United reached the final!

It was the old story. Once a team hits a bad patch it's difficult to get back on the rails again.

But there's no doubt there are players of talent at Maine Road. If they can put it all together Manchester City will soon be back among the trophies.

I certainly hope so. I came to Maine Road to improve myself—and to win the top honours in the game.

ASA HARTFORD
on the move

TORNADO

EARTH QUAKES
SAN JOSE

Quicksilvers
LAS VEGAS PROFESSIONAL
SOCCER CLUB

VANCOUVER
WHITECAPS

COSMOS

JERSEY
BADGES

American
Style

PORTLAND TIMBERS

L.A. AZTECS

ROWDIES

SEATTLE
SOUNDERS

St. LOUIS STARS
SOCCER CLUB

MINNESOTA
Kicks

METROS

CHICAGO
STING

Strikers

BICENTENNIALS

CONNECTICUT

ROCHESTER
LANCERS

TEAM HAWAII

DIPLOMATS
PRO. SOCCER

112

ROKER PARK RAIDER

The goal-scoring touch of Sunderland's GARY ROWELL took them to the brink of promotion last season.

A repeat of that form is a must if the Roker Park club are to clinch a First Division place.

Newcastle United's
ALAN SHOULDER
talking

FOR me Christmas came early a year ago. On Monday, December 4, to be exact.

That was when I signed as a full-time professional footballer with Newcastle United . . . at age 25!

That morning had begun like any other. At 10 a.m., however, I received a message to 'phone Newcastle manager Bill McGarry.

When I put through the call, Mr McGarry's request was simple. " Can you come to the ground sometime today and have a chat with me?"

We arranged to meet at 2 p.m. Only when I'd put the 'phone down did I realise I was due to start work as a miner at the coal-face, an hour after that appointment time!

There I explained the situation to my boss. And perhaps I've got to be thankful he is a United fan and season-ticket holder!

" Take the day off," he told me without hesitation. " And good luck, son!"

At 2 p.m. I walked into Mr McGarry's office. Less than five minutes later I'd signed the forms making me a Newcastle United player.

Mr McGarry has since said it must have been one of the easiest and quickest transfer deals ever.

With hardly a thought about the contract I was being offered, I almost snapped at him . . . " Give me the pen. I'll sign."

Then came a question that really rocked me. " How do you fancy playing against Stoke on Saturday?" asked Mr McGarry. " Think you'll be okay?"

Before I could reply, he answered the questions himself. " You'll need to be. You're definitely playing."

So began my career as a professional footballer. Six months that still seem like a dream.

ONCE-IN-A-LIFETIME

AT 25 I'd resigned myself to a career with Blyth Spartans in non-league football.

Even the tremendous local ' press ' coverage I'd had over the previous 12 months hadn't convinced me I was going to be handed such a late opportunity to make good.

That ' paper ' build-up had begun with the magnificent F.A. Cup run Spartans had the previous season. We'd reached the fifth round, beating top sides like Stoke on the way.

I always thought the highlight of my career would be the day we met Wrexham in that fifth round. A game that was televised as " Match of the Day."

I couldn't see anything ever topping that for me. It was a once-in-a-lifetime happening for a non-League player.

But, of course, all the glamour of that occasion was nothing compared to the unbelievable day I signed for Newcastle.

I doubt, also, whether I could have expected the

SUDDENLY I WAS IN AT THE DEEP END

events of the next few months to work out so well.

In the 24 League games I played for United last season I scored 11 goals. I also picked up one or two ' awards ' on the way.

I was voted Newcastle's joint Player-of-the-Year along with Peter Withe, who only 12 months before, had won a League Championship medal with Nottingham Forest and cost United £200,000.

It was an honour, too, to be voted North-East Sports Personality of the Year by the Newcastle Sport Council.

But perhaps the award that delighted me most was being voted ' My Favourite Magpie ' by the under-15s who follow Newcastle's fortunes from the terraces.

That really tickled me—to win the approval of all those kids.

SHATTERED

IT's been a fairy-tale. But, there is no way I'm ever likely to let myself get carried away by it all.

I can honestly say training for two hours has left me more shattered than a shift down the pit. At one time I'd probably never have believed that myself. But it is true.

What has greatly changed for me is being paid good money for keeping fit and playing the game I've always loved. I've also got more time to enjoy it.

For instance, in the two days before I signed for United, I played for Blyth Spartans on the Saturday afternoon and then did a shift down the mine at night.

The following morning I was looking out my gear again to play in the local Sunday League. I was shattered by the afternoon.

I've felt like that a few times since I joined Newcastle, too. But I'm now in the lucky position of having time to relax and recover my energy.

There have already been a lot of highlights for me. Maybe the main one was being accepted by the other Newcastle players.

As experienced professionals they could have been excused for regarding me with a certain suspicion on my arrival. But they went out of their way to welcome and help me.

It was, in fact, only towards the end of last season I discovered there had been one or two younger players at the club who doubted my ability.

One came up to me before a game and said . . . " You know, Alan, I didn't really think you'd cope with the change from non-League to League football. But I was wrong!"

I appreciated that so much.

I don't believe that the rest of my football career will be a bed of roses.

I'm going to suffer disappointments, that's for sure. But at very least, I'm now a professional footballer.

No matter what happens I'll consider every season I get out of the game a bonus.

PETE WITHE——Player of the year

KEEGAN'S CRACKER

After a run from the half way line and a brilliant one-two with Trevor Brooking, Kevin Keegan applied the killer touch as he beat Scotland's 'keeper, George Wood. A goal that was the highlight of the England v Scotland clash at Wembley.

HOW DID YOU SCORE?

ANSWERS TO PUZZLES ON PAGE 12

CROSSWORD

B	U	R	L	E	Y		O	F	F	S	E	T
O		A		V		S		I		M		O
L	E	I	C	E	S	T	E	R		I	R	K
T		D		N		O		S		T		E
O	W	E	N		K	I	T	C	H	E	N	
N		R		P	E	A						S
	A	S	T	L	E		R	I	V	A	L	
S			Y		S		D		R		A	
P	O	R	T	M	A	N		I	D	O	L	
I		A		O		I		S		I		A
R	E	D		U	N	P	O	P	U	L	A	R
I		I		T		S		U		E		M
T	R	O	P	H	Y		C	R	E	S	T	S

SPOT THE CLUES

1. SHREWSBURY TOWN. 2. MEADOWBANK THISTLE.
3. COLCHESTER UNITED. 4. BIRMINGHAM CITY.
5. CHARLTON ATHLETIC. 6. DONCASTER ROVERS.

NAME GAME

1. NELSON, 2. MARINER, 3. HARRIS, 4. HEIGHWAY,
5. JORDAN, 6. BURNS, 7. DURBAN, 8. VILLA, 9. CARR,
10. ROUGH, 11. COOPER.

SPOT THE TEAM

EVERTON.

FACE NAME

FRANCIS.

LETTER LINKS

SOUNESS, COPPELL, WILKINS, HEGARTY, CUNNINGHAM, NELSON, HARRIS.

S	I	S	R	E	N	M	I	N	U
E	O	R	A	L	A	N	N	C	Y
S	N	U	H	O	S	H	G	R	T
C	S	P	N	L	L	N	G	A	
O	P	E	L	W	K	I	S	H	E

WORD PYRAMID

			N					
		K	O	P				
	M	A	R	S	H			
S	T	E	W	A	R	T		
C	A	P	P	I	E	L	O	W
N	O	T	T	S	C	O	U	N	T	Y
W	O	L	V	E	R	H	A	M	P	T	O	N

117

HOW NOTTINGHAM

TREVOR FRANCIS—
Million pound match winner

THE British winter was still offering grey miserable weather in May when Nottingham Forest arrived at East Midlands airport to set off on their bid to win the European Cup.

In smart blue blazers and grey slacks they listened to reports that other planes had been diverted because of fierce cross winds.

Not a good start to the trip that was a fairy-tale come true for a club that had been in the bottom half of the Second Division only a couple of years earlier.

But soon they are given the all clear and the green and white Aer Lingus jet thunders down the runway on the first stage of the journey to Munich and the date with Swedish champions Malmo.

Just one hour and thirty minutes later skipper John McGovern is leading his men across the tarmac in Germany.

Manager Brian Clough is not with the party. Ever the unorthodox character, he is still on holiday in Crete, and will not join his players until evening.

Assistant Peter Taylor gives the first press conference while waiting for the baggage to be delivered.

Injuries to Frank Clark, Archie Gemmill and Martin O'Neill will force Forest to delay team choice.

BIG PROBLEM

TAYLOR tells the English pressmen the main problem will be to beat Malmo's offside trap.

"We have to get players to time their runs to the split second to open them up," he says.

Forest board the coach that is to take them to a hotel in the north of Munich.

Around four o'clock they go for a training session. No demands are made for the use of the stadium. They wander into a local park for a work-out watched by children.

After baths in their rooms, the players come down for an evening meal in the candle-lit dining room.

Steak or fish is the order for most. Follows a stroll around the neighbourhood on a warm balmy evening. By then manager Clough has joined the party.

Next morning Clough is off to play squash, his favourite pastime. He steals reserve 'keeper Chris Woods from the squad as partner.

The rest of the team go off to train. The Bavarian Alps high above the city are still white-capped with snow but the temperature on the training pitch is

A TALE

FOREST MADE A DREAM COME TRUE

THE GOAL THAT DID IT

soaring up towards the 80's.

Manager Clough reappears for a lunch-time press conference an hour late. Still in training gear and wiping the sweat from his brow, he predicts a close game, with Malmo proving awkward customers.

Down town in Munich the fans are beginning to arrive. 27,000 Forest enthusiasts will fly in decked out in their red and white colours. There are many fewer Swedish fans to parade their blue and white around the quaint spires and clock towers of the Bavarian capital.

The team are early abed. They will not train in the morning but all three injured players will face fitness tests.

At 11.30 managers Clough and Taylor lead their men into the Olympic Stadium—the stately home of Bayern Munich.

Out on the lush grass pitch they stare admiringly around the fabulous modern ground.

"You could play snooker on that pitch," says Brian Clough.

His team selection leaves out Archie Gemmill and Martin O'Neill. Million-pound signing Trevor Francis plays at number 7.

Back to the hotel for a light lunch and sleep. At 6 p.m. the party boards their coach—a gleaming Mercedes monster—to drive the five miles to the ground. This time a police escort, blue lights flashing and sirens howling, speeds them through the crowds.

A tumultuous welcome greets them as they step down to enter the dressing-rooms an hour before kick-off.

It is nothing to the explosion of noise that fills the night air as skipper John McGovern marches out at the head of the red line. The ground seems swamped by red-and-white banners.

Said winger John Robertson later, "It was an amazing sight. I have known days at Nottingham when there were less than 10,000 in the ground. Here we are hundreds of miles from home and all you could see was a huge bank of red. It made you feel so proud they had all taken the trouble to come over in support."

The game never hit the high level everyone had hoped would come from the final. Malmo soon made it obvious they had no intention of taking Forest on going for goals. They sat tight and played their offside trap for all it was worth.

Then, with injury time looming at the end of the first half, John Robertson set off down the left. For once he wriggled past his three-man guard and crossed to the far post.

There stood Malmo's executioner. Million-pound man Trevor Francis launched himself into the air to head home the goal that killed Swedish hopes.

Neutrals watching on TV back home found the goalless second half a disappointment.

Forest fans present thought otherwise. They knew how far their team had come in two years. They remembered the bad times.

" ALL YOU COULD SEE WAS A HUGE BANK OF RED "

Now the European Cup was within reach. Pent-up emotion sent the sound waves crashing around the Olympic bowl. Grown men and women wept with joy as the final whistle sounded triumph for Forest.

Skipper John McGovern stepped up to take the huge trophy and turned to thrust it skywards to yet another thunderous roll of acclaim.

Later, celebrating in the hotel, he was tell of that moment.

"Whatever else happens in my life, nobody can ever take that experience away from me," he said.

And so back into the jet next morning for a champagne flight to Nottingham. Thousands of fans crowded the terminal buildings to greet them. Half a million more would be in front of the town hall that night.

No, it wasn't a final to thrill the neutral. But to the people of Nottingham it was a dream come true. Their cheers and tears showed how very much it had all meant for them.

OF TRIUMPH

● ● ● IT HAPPENED

1 — Which team, down 0-2 at half-time in an F.A. Cup game, went on to win 1-0?

2 — **Name the first club to know it was promoted, and the first to know it was relegated.**

3 — One player's two-game suspension lasted from December 26 to February 21. Name, please.

4 — **The Scottish Cup-tie between Inverness Thistle and Falkirk suffered a record number of postponements. Was it 20, 25, 30 or 35?**

5 — Trevor Francis was the first million-pound player. Who was the first half-million-pound goalkeeper?

6 — **He set up a unique record when he won his second successive F.A. Cup medal in May. Name, please.**

7 — Which club outside the top two English divisions was the first to spend more than £200,000 on a player?

8 — **Who was elected Sportswriters' "Player of the Year"? Who won the P.F.A. "Player of the Year" award?**

22 TESTING

9 — He was the only home Scot in Scotland's team v. England at Wembley. Name and club, please.

10 — **Who was top goalscorer in the four English divisions? And what was his tally in League and Cup?**

11 — Osvaldo Ardiles and Ricardo Villa joined Spurs at the start of last season. Name two other Argentinians who came to England.

SNOWBALL

LAST SEASON ● ●

12 — Which two English First Division clubs met seven times last season?

13 — A Swansea City player fetched a record fee for a Third Division club when he moved to the First Division last season. Name player, new club and fee, please.

QUESTIONS

14 — What was the record margin of victory in the English First Division last season?

15 — 1978-79 saw the invasion of the foreign players. But only one reached a Wembley final. Player and club, please.

16 — The centre-backs in the Northern Ireland team against England at Wembley were related to each other. What were their names and how were they related?

17 — Ten Liverpool players were selected for the Home International Championship. One had never even played for the club. Who was he?

18 — A player started the season in the First Division, was transferred to a club relegated to the Second, then to one relegated to the Third. Who was he?

19 — Last season, for the first time ever, a player was sent off in a major Cup Final at Hampden Park. Name the player and the match.

20 — He scored four goals in only his second game for one of the home countries in this season's European Championships. Who was he?

21 — The Sportswriters' "Player of the Year" in Scotland was a free-transfer man from his first senior club. Who was he?

22 — Liverpool set a new record for League title wins last season. How often have they won the championship?

(Answers on page 125)

Out with the skis and sledges could have been the plea from the players in this Wolves v. Everton clash. But our footballers often have to face worse conditions than these . . .

happened I'd have been disappointed there was nothing to go along with it."

As well as building teams, former joiner McLean builds houses. He has just completed his third on on the outskirts of Dundee.

Considering he puts in around 12 hours a day on club duties in the playing season—seeming to get everywhere in search of players after a day at the ground—nobody can understand how he finds time to supervise his helpers on the building site.

THE TANGERINES

UNITED also have the distinction of a physiotherapist-team-attendant who was once a manager himself. For Andy Dickson spent three years as boss of Dunfermline Athletic.

'THE TERRORS' INTO 'THE

-after a spell

DAVID NAREY is tall and dark and as quiet as you make 'em.

But what a noise there was when Scotland capped him for a European Championship tie in Portugal last season.

Proud that David should bring them their first "full" international honour in 70 years of existence, his club, Dundee United, hoisted the Lion Rampant of Scotland on the flagpole atop their stand.

"You can't do that," came the indignant stricture from the Edinburgh office of the authorities concerned with heraldic matters. "And don't do it again."

So, when another United player, Paul Hegarty, became United internationalist No. 2, the flagpole remained bare.

Dundee United, a wee club that has grown to greatness, is seldom out of the news. And, last season, the news they made was mostly of great achievement.

For almost half the nine months of the Premier League competition they led the table—being overtaken only in the last lap by Celtic, who finished champions, and Rangers, the runners-up.

Marvellously, in company of clubs who spend hundreds of thousands on players, their third place was achieved with a side containing only two "bought men"—Hegarty, for £33,000 from Hamilton Accies, and George Fleming, who came from Hearts for £7000.

The others were products of the highly-respected coaching organisation set up by Jim McLean—the manager who admits he is never satisfied.

"I'd have given anything to have brought the League Championship Trophy to Tannadice Park," he said when accepting such success was beyond his team. "But I suppose if that had

DAVID NAREY—first " full " cap.

122

Then, in the Scottish League's official handbook, they list the only woman secretary in the Premier competition—the super-efficient Mrs Helen Lindsay, who mothers the ball-boy team on Saturdays.

She has her office in the modern steel and concrete stand that was opened in 1962—taking the place of a wooden edifice remembered nostalgically by old-timers.

Indeed, when it was about to be demolished, a veteran fan arrived to ask—" could he have his seat sawn out so he might take it home and set it up in his garden?"

The United people were happy to oblige . . .

Veteran of the United side that hit high spots last season was Hamish McAlpine, goalkeeper with 13 years service.

WHO TURNED TANGERINES' as 'UNDERTAKERS'

PAUL HEGARTY—bargain buy.

All-round sportsman Hamish is a crack shot, a low-handicap golfer, quite a cricketer—and a fellow who flavours his goalkeeping with the unorthodox.

He even scored a batch of important penalties for the team.

Formerly known as " The Tannadice Terrors ", United have become " The Tangerines " since shifting to that colour from combinations of black and white.

Once they had a set of black jerseys with white edgings. But that was a mistake in ordering. It should have been the other way round.

Making use of the gear once or twice, United got themselves talked about and nick-named by some fans as " Undertakers ".

They have certainly undertaken a lot of distant travel over the past few years.

All around the Continent. To Mexico in that country's World Cup year of 1970. To Nigeria and North Korea for games with clubs away off the beaten track.

Then, when the North American Soccer League was set-up in 1967, United went out to Texas and played as Dallas Tornado for a few weeks.

And so to last close-season, which brought them a fortnight in Japan—taking part in an invitation and only being beaten in the final by Spurs.

So to join United is to see the world.

JIM McLEAN—hard working manager.

BRENDAN O'CALLAGHAN
Stoke City
and Eire

◆ ◆ YOUR PICTURE GUIDE ◆ ◆

QUIZ ANSWERS — From pages 122-123

1—Oldham Athletic. Their third round tie with Stoke was abandoned at half-time with Stoke leading 2—0. Oldham won the re-arranged game 1—0.

2—Grimsby Town. Chelsea.

3—Joey Jones of Wrexham. Bad weather restricted the Welsh club to only two games in that period.

4—Thirty.

5—Phil Parkes. He moved from Q.P.R. to West Ham for £560,000.

6—Brian Talbot. He was the first to win two successive winners' medals with two different clubs.

7—Watford paid £200,000 for Leicester's Steve Sims.

8—Kenny Dalglish of Liverpool. Liam Brady of Arsenal.

9—Paul Hegarty, Dundee United.

10—Ross Jenkins of Watford with 38.

11—Alex Sabella, Sheffield United. Alberto Tarantini, Birmingham City.

12—Leeds United and West Bromwich Albion. They met twice in the League, twice in the F.A. Cup and three times in the League Cup.

13—Alan Curtis, Leeds United. £400,000.

14—Liverpool beat Tottenham Hotspur 7—0 at Anfield.

15—Ivan Golac. The Yugoslav played for Southampton in the League Cup final against Nottingham Forest.

16—Jimmy Nicholl of Manchester United and Southampton's Chris Nicholl. They are cousins.

17—Frank McGarvey, signed from St Mirren just before the season's end, was in Scotland's squad.

18—Duncan McKenzie. He started with Everton, moved to Chelsea, then on to Blackburn Rovers.

19—Doug Rougvie. The Aberdeen defender was ordered off in the League Cup Final against Rangers.

20—Ian Edwards of Chester and Wales. He scored four against Malta at the Racecourse Ground, Wrexham.

21—Andy Ritchie, Morton. Celtic released him.

22—Eleven.

Printed and published by D. C. Thomson & Co. Ltd., 185 Fleet Street, London EC4A 2HS.
© D. C. Thomson & Co. Ltd., 1979.